1. *Henrietta Maria*, by an unknown artist.
(National Portrait Gallery, London)

GREAT PERIODS OF THE BRITISH MONARCHY

National Portrait Gallery, London

# Henrietta Maria
## the Intrepid Queen

## ROSALIND K. MARSHALL

Stemmer
House
PUBLISHERS, INC.

Owings Mills, Maryland

Text copyright © 1990 by Rosalind K. Marshall
First published by HMSO, London, England, 1990
First published in the USA by Stemmer House Publishers, Inc.,
Owings Mills, Maryland, 1991

Inquiries should be directed to
Stemmer House Publishers, Inc.
2627 Caves Road
Owings Mills, Maryland 21117

*A Barbara Holdridge book*

Printed and bound in Great Britain

**Library of Congress Cataloging-in-Publication Data**

Marshall, Rosalind K.
 Henrietta Maria, the intrepid queen / Rosalind K. Marshall.
  p.   cm. −− (Great periods of the British monarchy)
 Includes bibliographical references.
 ISBN 0−88045−117−3
  1. Henrietta Maria, Queen, consort of Charles I, King of
England, 1609−1669.  2. Great Britain −− History −− Charles I,
1625−1649.   3. Great Britain −− History −− Charles II, 1660−1685.
4. Great Britain −− Queens −− Biography,  I. Title,  II. Series.
DA396.A5M35 1990
941.06'2'092−−dc20
[B]                                                      90−44588
ISBN 0−88045−118−1                                          CIP

# CONTENTS

# ACKNOWLEDGMENTS

I should like to thank Professor Gordon Donaldson CBE, HM Historiographer in Scotland, who kindly read the completed text of this book. Professor C A Mayer and Dana Bentley-Cranch (Mrs Mayer) generously interrupted their own researches in Paris and London to pursue elusive documents for me, Mrs Mayer in addition providing expert guidance on French iconographic sources. I am most grateful to them and to the staff of HMSO, particularly Philip Glover, Assistant Director, for his helpful efficiency, and Gavin Turner, initiator of this series of publications, for his continued interest and encouragement.

Dr Bernard Lunan of Glasgow Royal Maternity Hospital diagnosed Henrietta's serious illness, and I have also received valuable assistance from Hugh Roberts, Deputy Surveyor of The Queen's Works of Art, and the staff of The Royal Collection, Tess Wright, Dr David Breeze, Priscilla Minay, Dr May Williamson, Diana Scarisbrick, Dr Helen Roberts, Valerie Cumming, Judith Prendergast of the National Portrait Gallery, Robert Blow of the National Buildings Record, Christopher Gatiss of the Courtauld Institute, Mrs Patricia Kennedy, Administrator at Parham Park, Dr May Prior, Ursula MacMullan of The Mansell Collection Ltd and A D Mitchell, Director of Tourism and Leisure Services, East Yorkshire Borough Council. Finally, I would thank the owners of all the items which appear as illustrations: individual acknowledgments are to be found in the captions.

RKM
Edinburgh, August 1989

# AUTHOR'S NOTE

Throughout her life, Henrietta Maria used both her names in the French form, 'Henriette Marie', but for the sake of brevity I have termed her 'Henrietta'. Charles I was officially styled King of England, France, Scotland and Ireland. Although the crowns of England and Scotland were united, each country still had its own parliament. There was therefore no British foreign policy as such, and English and Scottish interests often diverged. For this reason the text refers specifically to 'the English parliament', 'the Scottish parliament', and 'English foreign policy', as appropriate.

In the interests of clarity, I have modernised seventeenth-century spelling and punctuation and translated French into English. England still used the Old Style Julian calendar and was ten days behind the New Style adopted by France. I have therefore used New Style when Henrietta was on the Continent, Old Style when she was in England.

2. *Henry IV, King of France*, by Frans Pourbus.
(The Louvre, Paris: photograph, agraci, R M Jourdain)

# 1

## KING HENRY'S DAUGHTER

ON 8 JUNE 1625, Henrietta Maria stood on the shore at Boulogne, staring across the Channel. A small, determined figure, she was plainly but richly dressed, as befitted the daughter of a great French king. She had big dark eyes in a round face, curly brown hair, very white skin and excellent if rather protruding teeth. Vivacious and full of energy, she was rarely still, but now she stood motionless, lost in thought, her gaze fixed on the hazy outline of the English coast. Her courtiers strolled about the beach nearby, chattering animatedly to each other, growing restive, but no one dared to approach her. They knew only too well the fierce scowl and the sharp words that would greet any interruption. She was only fifteen, but she was imperious and well-used to command.

As they watched, the waves began to lap round her feet, but still she did not notice. Only when the water flowed over her shoes did she glance down. She smiled then, and turned away, apparently satisfied. It was a fine evening. If the weather held, she would sail next day for Dover. Waiting for her on the other side would be Charles I, King of England, Scotland, and Ireland, the husband she had never met.

The prospect was a daunting one, but she was not afraid. As she walked back to her lodgings, laughing and joking with her attendants, they could see that she was looking forward eagerly to her new life. She had been trained from early childhood for her future role as a queen. She knew what was expected. With a long letter of advice from her mother tucked safely away in her bodice, she was ready for anything and in many respects it would be almost a relief to leave behind the dramas and dissensions of the turbulent French court.

Henrietta had been born in Paris on 26 November 1609, the youngest child of the heroic King Henry IV of France and his second wife, Marie de Medici. Henry was fifty-seven by then, and his early faun-like elegance had given way to the raffish look of an ageing satyr. He had originally been King of Navarre, but he had succeeded to the French throne after converting to Roman Catholicism with the memorable words 'Paris is worth a Mass' and he had ruled successfully ever since. Treating his subjects with a mixture of toughness and uninhibited good humour, he was constantly on the move, replanning Paris, commissioning new buildings, clambering about the scaffolding to inspect the masons' work and pursuing a long series of beautiful women.

His wife witnessed his amorous exploits with seething rage. She was only half his age and she came from a wealthy Florentine family. He had married her for her money, of course, and when she first stepped ashore from the magnificent gold and jewel-encrusted galley which brought her from Italy, the French were much impressed. She was large, blonde and glittering with diamonds. Henry was delighted with her and she liked him, but their initial satisfaction was shortlived. The very day after they met he went off to visit his current mistress, and Marie realised to her fury that she was expected to share him not only with his numerous illegitimate children but with the witty, malicious Marchioness de Vermeil. From that moment on, the royal apartments rang with noisy quarrels, weary courtiers were constantly called upon

3. *Henry IV, his mistress Gabrielle d'Estrées and their illegitimate children, César and Catherine,* engraved in 1602.
(Bibliothèque Nationale, Paris)

to mediate, and the only time there was any peace was when the King and Queen were not on speaking terms.

Within a year of the wedding, Marie did her duty and presented her husband with a son and heir, the Dauphin Louis. Two more sons and two daughters followed. Henry doted on them. He loved all children and he decreed that his offspring, legitimate and illegitimate, should be brought up together. The Castle of St Germain, outside Paris, became their nursery and he visited them often, spending hours playing with them, indulging them one moment and rebuking them sternly the next. Marie de Medici objected to the St Germain arrangement. She hated her precious sons and daughters associating with the Marchioness de Vermeil's brats but, as always, Henry had his own way. Ignoring her protests, he simply told her that they needed more sons. He wanted to found a dynasty.

In the spring of 1609 she found that she was pregnant again. She spent that summer in the Louvre, the principal royal residence, reclining on her day-bed, complaining loudly of indigestion and bewailing her husband's unreasonable behaviour. When autumn came, her magnificent first-floor audience chamber was prepared for her confinement. Sumptuously furnished under her personal supervision, it had walls painted with delicate arabesques and a rich oriental carpet on the floor. The large armchairs were upholstered in crimson velvet and there were matching stools and couches, as well as elegant cabinets and little tables. A door in one corner led to the tower room, where a handsome carved cradle awaited the new baby.

When her pains began soon after five o'clock on the afternoon of 26 November, the two ladies who were with her hurried to fetch the midwife. Louise Bourgeois had delivered all Marie's children and she had been in the palace for some weeks already, in case of a premature birth. Now she came

2

4. *Louise Bourgeois*, the midwife who delivered Henrietta; from a seventeenth-century engraving in *Les Six Couches de Marie de Medicis* (Paris 1875).
(The British Library, 1581.a.1)

bustling in, grumbling about the inconvenience and expense. She had been forced to turn away dozens of clients as she waited about for this latest royal infant, she claimed, and she was determined to be recompensed. Soon everyone in the household knew what was happening. The King came hurrying through from his adjoining suite and the eight-year-old Dauphin arrived at the door of his mother's room, asking to be allowed in. 'Not yet', said Henry, and sent him away again.

Beneath the four magnificent silver-gilt chandeliers, Louise went to work. The Queen's sixth labour was swift and uncomplicated. Henrietta arrived just after ten o'clock that same night. Louise washed her in wine and oil of roses and placed her in her father's arms. He looked at her with exasperation. He did not want another girl. If she had been a boy, he would have distributed 100,000 livres to the poor, he exclaimed, and when Louise protested that he had paid her less than last time, he retorted briskly, 'You have to give more for sons than for daughters!'

His irritation soon passed. Everyone remarked that this new baby looked very like him and she provided a welcome diversion. He was feeling depressed that winter, weighed down by cares of state and plagued by his wife nagging at him to arrange her coronation. She had been in France for nearly ten years, she reminded him sourly, and she was the mother of three of his sons. How many more did he need before he was willing to recognise her officially as his consort?

He gave way in the end. He was planning to lead his army in a new war and while he was away she woud have to act as Regent. She was always saying that she would never manage, but perhaps if she were crowned she would have more confidence. The ceremony was planned for 13 May 1610, and that day all the children were taken to the Abbey Church of St Denis, even six-month-old Henrietta, carried in the arms of a high-born lady. The coronation went well: for once Marie was satisfied, and Henry was even heard to declare magnanimously that he had never seen her look more handsome.

The following afternoon, he decided to go for a drive through Paris. He would visit his leading adviser, the Duke de Sully, who was lying ill in his mansion on the other side of the city. On the way, he could inspect the decorations which were being put up for the Queen's state entry into the capital. Taking several of his gentlemen with him, he summoned his coach and off they went.

3

5. *The Coronation of Marie de Medici*, detail, painted for her Luxembourg Palace by Sir Peter Paul Rubens.
(The Louvre, Paris: photograph, Lauros-Giraudon)

The narrow streets were thronged with people so that it was difficult to get through, and as they were about to turn out of the Rue St Honoré they came to a halt. Most of the footmen hurried on ahead to clear the crowds out of the way. In that moment, a man sprang up as if from nowhere, put his foot on the wheel of the coach, drew a dagger from his cloak, leaned in at the window and stabbed the King in the chest. Henry had been reading a letter. 'I am wounded!' he gasped, falling back, and under the horrified eyes of his companions, the attacker struck again. 'It is nothing', the King moaned faintly as his eyes closed. The Duke d'Epérnon managed to deflect a third blow, but it was too late. Blood was everywhere. The King was dead, murdered by a deranged former monk named Ravaillac. Marie de Medici now became Regent for young Louis XIII.

Henrietta was taken to cast holy water on her father's body as it lay in state in the Louvre, and she attended his funeral at St Denis. After that, she went to St Germain to join the rest of the family. Louis would live in Paris with their mother now, but the other children were still in the nurseries: seven-year-old Elisabeth, dark and pretty; fair-haired, sturdy Christine, who was three, and the two boys. The little Duke d'Orleans at two was sadly delicate, with a huge head on a puny body. He suffered from hydrocephalus and he was rarely able

6. St. Germain, Henrietta's childhood home. The terraced gardens can clearly be seen in this painting of 1665 by A F Van Der Meulen.
(Carnavalet Museum, Paris: photograph, Lauros-Giraudon)

to leave his room. Indeed, he was never formally baptised and so his first name is unknown. Gaston, just a year older than Henrietta, was fortunately strong and lively, and he was his mother's favourite. As for the illegitimate family, the half-brothers were with the new King and only the Marchioness de Vermeil's daughter was left, a gentle little girl whom they all liked, in spite of her parentage.

The old castle, where they stayed, was a handsome building set among woodlands on the banks of the Seine. It had been erected about fifty years before. To the east, across the park and the bowling green, lay the new castle, little more than a summer pavilion, with apartments for their mother when she came to visit. Such occasions were rare, of course, because she was wrestling with the problems of ruling the country. Nervous of her new role at first, she had soon come to enjoy the exercise of power and with the help of Henry's advisers she was proving more effective than any of them would have imagined.

In her absence she delegated the daily care of her young family to her distant cousin, the Marchioness de Montglat. Known to the children as 'Mamanga', the Marchioness was a tall, thin lady who ruled over her complicated household with firm determination. She had no easy task. Each child possessed a personal retinue of attendants and so there were governesses,

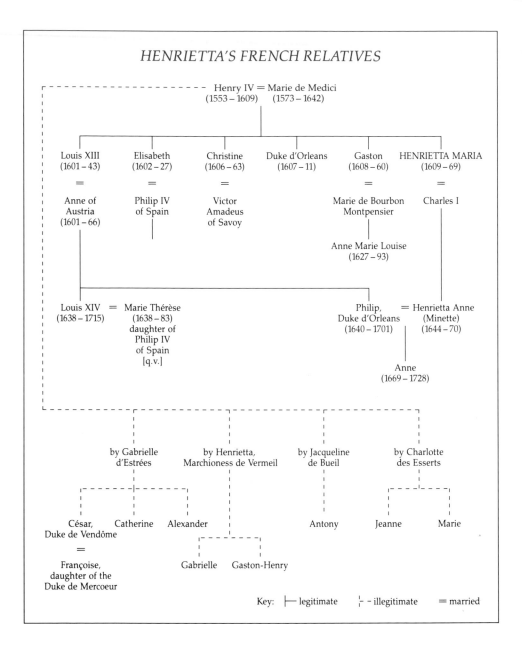

# HENRIETTA'S FRENCH RELATIVES

Henry IV = Marie de Medici
(1553 – 1609)  (1573 – 1642)

| Louis XIII | Elisabeth | Christine | Duke d'Orleans | Gaston | HENRIETTA MARIA |
|---|---|---|---|---|---|
| (1601 – 43) | (1602 – 27) | (1606 – 63) | (1607 – 11) | (1608 – 60) | (1609 – 69) |
| = | = | = | | = | = |
| Anne of Austria (1601 – 66) | Philip IV of Spain | Victor Amadeus of Savoy | | Marie de Bourbon Montpensier | Charles I |

Anne Marie Louise
(1627 – 93)

Louis XIV = Marie Thérèse
(1638 – 1715)  (1638 – 83)
daughter of
Philip IV
of Spain
[q.v.]

Philip, = Henrietta Anne
Duke d'Orleans  (Minette)
(1640 – 1701)  (1644 – 70)

Anne
(1669 – 1728)

by Gabrielle d'Estrées | by Henrietta, Marchioness de Vermeil | by Jacqueline de Bueil | by Charlotte des Esserts

César, Duke de Vendôme   Catherine   Alexander   Antony   Jeanne   Marie

=

Françoise, daughter of the Duke de Mercoeur

Gabrielle   Gaston-Henry

Key:  ⊢ legitimate  ⊢ - illegitimate  = married

---

nursemaids, dressers, footmen, tailors, doctors, musicians and pages as well as the cooks, guards, grooms and gardeners attached to the castle itself.

When Henrietta first arrived at St Germain she was in the care of her wet-nurse, Maman Dondon, but as she grew older Mamanga's daughter Jeanne looked after her. Jeanne was young, pretty and sympathetic, and the princesses were all fond of her. The Marchioness remained the ultimate authority, of course, responsible for discipline, and Henrietta's earliest surviving letter is addressed to her. 'Mamanga', she wrote, 'I pray you excuse me if you saw my little sulky fit which I had this morning. I cannot be good all of a sudden, but I will do all I can to content you, meantime I beg you will no longer be angry with me, who am and will be all my life, Mamanga, Your affectionate friend, Henrietta.'

7. *Henrietta in early childhood,*
by an unknown artist.
(In a private collection)

8. *Marie de Medici, Queen Regent, with her
son, Louis XIII,* by a seventeenth-century
engraver.
(Bibliothèque Nationale, Paris)

Even as a toddler she possessed a strong will. She might be the youngest member of the family, but she was determined not to be left out. She sang songs with the others, dressed up, danced, cooked sweetmeats in silver pans, raced about the rooms, chattered to the servants and played with the family pets. Marie de Medici was a great animal-lover and in each of her residences she kept a menagerie of dogs, monkeys and parakeets.

In summer, the children spent long hours in the beautiful terraced gardens sloping down to the Seine. These were justly famous for their many unusual features, and people came from far and near to admire them. There was an ornate fountain with a jet of water that soared to the height of two men and then splashed down again with a noise like musket-fire. There were peaches and quinces. Roses twined round trellises, trees shaded pleasant walks and, at the edge of the river, long borders were full of brightly-coloured flowers.

Most exciting of all were the marvellous grottoes constructed by an Italian engineer on the orders of Henry IV. Beneath the flights of steps linking the terraces, mechanical nightingales flapped their wings and sang, smiths struck anvils, water organs played, imitation lizards basked on rocks, and Neptune in his chariot rose from the centre of a great pool, turned right round and disappeared again beneath the surface of the waves.

The children delighted in turning on the fountains to soak unwary visitors and trying to slip unnoticed into the forbidden territory of their mother's private orchard. Often callers came. The local people were always in and about the castle on business, and they were easily persuaded to perform peasant dances for the amusement of the little princes and princesses. Sometimes there were more important guests, for Marie de Medici liked to send foreign ambassadors and other dignitaries to admire her family.

At intervals, Louis XIII himself appeared. A thin, dark, repressed boy who had shrunk from his father's robust teasing, he was growing every day more morose and withdrawn in the overpowering presence of his mother. He turned to his dogs for companionship, addressing them in a special language of his devising, and his only other pleasure was in revisiting the scene of his own early childhood. He usually arrived in time to take supper with his younger brothers and sisters, but the atmosphere was hardly relaxed or

9. The Louvre, the principal royal residence, engraved by Aveline.
(Bibliothèque Nationale, Paris)

informal. They had been taught to treat him with great deference. To Henrietta, he was always a rather distant figure: the King, rather than a loving relative.

Occasionally, they went to see him. Their mother was terrified that they might catch some of the diseases which were rife in the capital and after the little Duke d'Orleans died at the age of four she was even more anxious. They did have to attend state ceremonies, however, and on those occasions Henrietta was brought back to the palace where she had been born. The Louvre was a huge, rambling building, almost a town in itself. The children had their own nurseries, of course, but each day they were taken to the Queen Mother's suite to watch her dine in state and see splendidly-dressed courtiers stoop to kiss the hem of her dress.

The most sumptuous apartment of all was her bedchamber. Her enormous bed, hung with crimson velvet in winter and crimson silk in summer, stood on a low platform surrounded by a silver balustrade. Only the Queen herself and

10. Mirror belonging to Marie de Medici. Made of rock crystal in a gold frame set with agates, sardonyx and precious stones, it was a wedding present to her from Venice.
(The Louvre, Paris: photograph, Bulloz)

11. *Leonora Galigai*, Marie de Medici's childhood friend and confidante, by an unknown artist, 1614.
(Bibliothèque Nationale, Paris)

her very personal servants were allowed to open the little gate and go in to this most private part of the room. Portraits of the Medici family and ornate mirrors hung on the walls, torches blazed in silver sconces and her ebony and japanned cabinets were crammed with treasures: rare porcelain, Venetian crystal, gold medals, diamond-studded reliquaries and statues of the saints.

Henrietta grew up accepting all this magnificence as the appropriate setting for a monarch, and she was equally accustomed to the vast numbers of people who came to the palace: noblemen, ambassadors, servants in blue and white liveries, poor men and women with petitions and sightseers from foreign lands. In all, there were almost five hundred men and women in the Queen's household, ranging from the chevalier of honour who escorted her on public occasions to the *valets-de-chambre* who came in each morning at five in winter to light the fires and the candles. The King had a complete household of his own.

Many of the courtiers were old friends, like the Baron de Bassompierre, who had been Henry IV's trusted companion and was now one of the Queen's Gentlemen of the Bedchamber. Marie's closest advisers were two Italians who had come with her from Florence, ugly little Leonora Galigai and her unlikely husband, the handsome, swaggering Concino Concini. The French hated them. Concini had far too much influence over the Queen, they complained, and Leonora not only looked after Marie's jewels but was closeted with her each night, retailing all the gossip of the court.

The Queen also had ten maids of honour, high-born girls looking for husbands, as well as Madeleine the Moor, Mathurine the Fool, and a number of more lowly chamberwomen. Fifty priests looked after her spiritual welfare and five resident doctors and two surgeons tended the physical health of herself and her children. When Henrietta suffered from one of her recurring bouts of fever, Dr Paulin was sent to examine her. Forty cooks prepared meals for Marie and her nobles, while another forty cooked for the servants. There were fruiterers, bakers, butlers and cellarers, and of course the stables had a full complement of grooms, coachmen and footmen. Hunting was Marie's favourite sport and she made sure that all the children learned to ride at an

early age. For less strenuous outings, they went out together in her heavy gilt coach lined with red velvet, she and her daughters wearing fancy masks, as etiquette demanded.

Public appearances held no fears for Henrietta and at the age of three she played a leading part in one such court ceremony, when she and Gaston were christened. They had both been baptised privately a few days after birth but, according to royal custom, the public naming waited until they were old enough to understand what was happening. Marie de Medici's Grand Almoner, Cardinal de Bonsi, officiated in her private chapel in the Louvre, with Princess Elisabeth and the Cardinal de la Rochefoucauld acting as Henrietta's godparents.

During those early years her life had a settled pattern, but when she was four and a half her world began to change. Louis had his thirteenth birthday, which meant that he came of age officially. There were pageants, processions and bonfires, and Henrietta sat near the throne in Notre Dame Cathedral when he made a speech promising to be a just and merciful monarch. He was not old enough to rule for himself, of course, but his mother decided that the time had come for him to take a wife. In a surprising diplomatic coup, she arranged that he and Elisabeth should marry the son and daughter of France's old enemy, the King of Spain. She hoped that this would safeguard the country from any attack from the south, and it also fulfilled part of a cherished personal ambition. She was determined that all her daughters should one day be queens.

There were more lavish celebrations, and the children's dismay at the prospect of losing Elisabeth was soon forgotten in a new excitement. The entire court would go to the Spanish border to exchange the Princess for the Infanta, and Christine, Gaston and Henrietta would go too. They set out in August 1615, their cavalcade making slow progress through the countryside as every town and village welcomed them with pageants, gifts and congratulatory addresses.

On the way, Marie de Medici fell ill and they had to stop at Poitiers where, to the horror of them all, Elisabeth caught smallpox. For some days her life was in danger but mercifully she recovered. Her beauty unimpaired, she sailed in

13. *The Double Marriage of Louis XIII and Princess Elisabeth*, to Anne of Austria and the future Philip IV of Spain. Marie de Medici and her children are on the left. (Bibliothèque Nationale, Paris)

triumph into Bordeaux in the royal barge, with her mother, Henrietta and Christine at her side. They said goodbye to her there and a few days later they greeted the Infanta.

Anne of Austria was a tall, well-made fifteen-year-old in a green silk dress, a green velvet cap perched on her fair ringlets. She was an amiable, kindhearted girl, but her new family greeted her with reserve. Louis had no interest in women and his mother was determined that she was not going to take second place to anyone. Indeed, she did all she could to stir up trouble between the young couple and, at her instigation, Henrietta and Christine played mischievous tricks on the newcomer.

The journey back to Paris was a nightmare for them all. The weather was bitterly cold and the roads were bad. Sickness broke out among the soldiers who were escorting them and men died by the roadside every day. Bored and out of sorts, Marie de Medici was in the worst possible humour and Anne's Spanish attendants bickered constantly with the French royal household. When at last they came within reach of Paris, Marie took her two daughters and rode hastily ahead to the capital.

It was May now. They had been away for nearly ten months. Henrietta and Christine consoled themselves for Elisabeth's absence by sending her letters and little presents. She reciprocated with a gift of dolls' clothing for Henrietta. Marie de Medici in the meantime had been forced to vacate her magnificent apartments in the Louvre. They were the official lodgings of the Queen of France and so Anne had to have them. With an ill grace, Marie moved down to

11

14. *Princess Elisabeth*, Henrietta's sister, by an unknown Spanish artist, about 1620. (Museo del Prado, Madrid)

the ground floor and took a petty revenge by sending all her daughter-in-law's personal servants back to Spain.

More serious troubles were looming too. For years her son Louis had been smouldering with resentment and now, urged on by his friend Charles de Luynes, a falconer in his household, he decided to oust his mother and the insufferable Concini. On 24 April 1617, as Concini strutted across the courtyard of the Louvre, he was suddenly surrounded by a party of royal guards. Before he could utter a word of protest, a volley of shots rang out and he fell, dying, to the ground. Servants and courtiers came running to see what had happened, a window high up above them opened and Louis appeared. 'Now I really am a King!' he shouted triumphantly. Shortly afterwards, Leonora was dragged away to be burned as a witch.

Henrietta, Gaston and Christine were in the palace when all this took place, and for several days Louis forbade them to see their mother. Finally, they were taken to her apartments to find her clad in her habitual black, in floods of tears. She had agreed to live in exile outside Paris and she was about to depart. When the King arrived to see her off there was a stormy scene and she begged to be allowed to take Henrietta with her. Reluctantly, Louis agreed, and mother and daughter set off in a coach together through crowds of silent spectators.

For the next two years they were virtual prisoners in the Castle of Blois, comfortably enough accommodated but surrounded by spies and forbidden to leave. When Marie heard that Louis was planning to marry Christine to the

15. *Charles de Luynes*, favourite of Louis XIII, by an unknown engraver.
(Scottish National Portrait Gallery)

Duke of Savoy's son, she decided that she could stand it no longer. She intended her second daughter for the King of England's heir. Something would have to be done. Late one night, she clambered through her closet window, high up in the castle. This was no easy matter for one of her ample proportions and for a dreadful moment she was stuck. After a desperate struggle she wriggled free, only to panic halfway down the long ladders. She clung there in terror, unable to move, until her companions managed to wrap her in her cloak and lower her to the ground. Somehow or other all this activity went unnoticed and she rode away to a rendezvous with some of her supporters.

She was too late to prevent the wedding. It had taken place eleven days before. Christine was charmed with her personable young bridegroom and Louis was preparing to escort them to the Italian border. He was disgusted when he heard that his mother had escaped, but his courtiers persuaded him that his quarrel with her was most unseemly and he agreed to make it up. Henrietta attended the grand, twelve-day festival of reconciliation with the rest of the family, and then Louis took her away with him on the trip towards Savoy. She had spent long enough in her mother's company, he thought. Eventually, they all arrived back in Paris. After much wrangling, Louis and Marie de Medici finally agreed to rule together, assisted by her protégé, the able young Cardinal Richelieu.

The King now took Gaston on a campaign against the Huguenots. Because of the privileges his father had granted these Protestant subjects, Louis feared that they were becoming far too powerful, in danger of forming a state within a state. That could never be allowed. Henrietta in the meantime stayed with her mother in Paris. Her rooms in the Louvre were next to Marie's on the ground floor, overlooking a pleasant garden. She was nine years old now, and in all the recent turmoil her education had been sadly neglected. For a time she and Gaston had shared a tutor, Monsieur de Brèves. An expert in oriental literature, he had probably not been the best person to instruct that high-spirited pair and he soon departed. Marie de Medici was not particularly upset. She had no interest in producing learned daughters. Henrietta had to learn to read and write, of course, but otherwise it was far more important that she should sing and dance well, for those were the skills she would need in later life.

13

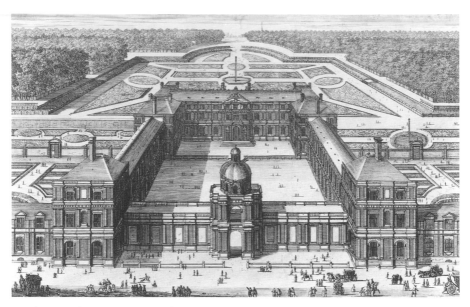

16. *The Luxembourg Palace*, built for Marie de Medici. This view is by an unknown engraver. (Bibliothèque Nationale, Paris)

Religious instruction mattered, too. Personally devout, the Queen Mother made sure that Henrietta attended Mass each day, and she put Madame Madeleine de St Joseph, a Carmelite, in charge of her spiritual education. Marie liked to walk in the grounds of the Carmelite Convent in the Faubourg St Jacques and Henrietta began to spend weeks at a time there with the nuns, apparently enjoying their tranquil company.

Back in the palace, life was never calm, but it was certainly interesting. The proud possessor of a magnificent collection of jewels, Marie de Medici knew all about gems and she frequently bought new pieces. Her daughter watched in fascination as she haggled with the merchants over the value. Soon Henrietta had her own goldsmith to look after her necklaces and earrings. She also came to share her mother's enthusiasm for interior decoration. Horrified on her arrival in France at the shabby appearance of the Louvre, Marie had long since resolved to make improvements, and as well as purchasing fine furniture, she imported Greek and Turkish embroideresses to sew soft furnishings. Some of these girls married into local families and one or two eventually entered the Carmelite nunnery.

By the time Henrietta was growing up there was an even more ambitious project in hand. Marie had decided to build herself a fine new palace on the site of the Duke de Luxembourg's house and it was now nearing completion. The celebrated artist Peter Paul Rubens and his assistant Anthony Van Dyck were busy painting a series of murals depicting a somewhat idealised version of the main events in her life, and Henrietta went with her regularly to see how work was progressing. Naturally, the pictures evoked vivid memories and the Queen told Henrietta all about her journey to France and her years of marriage. Now that Henry IV had gone she had quite forgotten his more tiresome characteristics and she boasted proudly of all his achievements. Henrietta loved to hear these stories, and throughout her life she was extremely proud of the fact that she was the daughter of the remarkable Henry the Victorious.

17. *Marie de Medici*, drawn in about 1625
by Rubens, while he was decorating
the Luxembourg Palace for her.
(The Louvre, Paris: photograph,
Lauros-Giraudon)

Sometimes, during their visits to the Luxembourg Palace, the workmen would lay on special oboe concerts for them. The royal ladies' love of music was well-known. The Queen Mother had her own group of singers and instrumentalists, led by the composer, Pierre de Guedron. She often borrowed famous singers from Italy to perform for her and she was quick to employ any accomplished musicians who happened to be passing through Paris. Henrietta had a beautiful singing voice, and music was a great source of pleasure for her.

She and her mother also shared a love of the theatre. An avid playgoer herself, Marie liked nothing better than to spend an evening at the Italian comedy and her bored courtiers noticed that she laughed louder than anyone else in the audience. Sometimes she had taken Louis with her, but Henrietta was a much more appreciative companion. Better still were the court masques. These were elaborate affairs, involving singing, dancing, acting and amazing stage effects. Thanks to the ingenuity of Italian engineers, imitation waves rose and fell, rocks emerged from the ground and clouds descended from the heavens bearing angelic choirs. At one time the Queen Mother had been an energetic performer, but now she left it to her daughter. Henrietta's lovely voice was a great asset and she was a graceful dancer.

In January 1623, she was happily engaged in rehearsals for a new masque. Louis XIII had won another victory over the Huguenots and in celebration he would make a state entry into Paris. This latest performance was to be part of the entertainment. Henrietta was not particularly fond of her brother: no one was. Gloomy and morose, he had few friends and he and his wife had been on worse terms than ever since she had suffered a miscarriage. It was her own fault for being so careless, he told her unsympathetically, and he was refusing to have any more to do with her. However, appearances must be maintained, and when the masque was suggested Anne agreed to play the leading role of Juno, Queen of the gods, with Henrietta as her handmaiden Iris.

Practising in a large, rather dimly-lit hall in the Louvre, Henrietta danced 'rarely well', according to the courtiers who looked in to watch. Indeed, she was so busy concentrating on the intricate steps of the dance that she paid no heed when two oddly-dressed strangers joined the spectators. One was very tall and broad-shouldered, the other small and slight. Both wore shabby clothes and very large, bushy wigs. They stood and watched for a time, questioning a companion about the identity of the performers, and then they slipped away. No one had recognised Charles, Prince of Wales and his friend George Villiers, Duke of Buckingham.

# 2

## THE PRINCE'S BRIDE

*I*T WAS impossible to keep anything secret at the French court, and within hours the whole of Paris was buzzing with excited speculation. What could it mean? No royal prince, heir to an ancient throne, would normally hazard himself by travelling abroad incognito. There could be only one possible explanation, the courtiers told each other. He had come to take a private look at Henrietta because he wanted her for his wife.

Marie de Medici was jubilant, but no sooner had her hopes been raised than they were cruelly dashed again. Instead of making themselves known and seeking an audience with her, the travellers vanished. They were last seen at three o'clock in the morning, riding for the Spanish border. Far from inspecting Henrietta, Charles had hardly noticed her. He was going to Madrid to woo the King of Spain's daughter.

The French were affronted. It was a pity, said Anne of Austria, that the Prince had seen Henrietta from a distance and in such a poor light. If he had viewed her more closely, he would have seen how lovely she was and he might have changed his plans. It was even more of a pity, retorted Henrietta,

18. *Charles I*, on the eve of his visit to Spain, by Daniel Mytens.
(On loan to the Scottish National Portrait Gallery from the Earl of Mar and Kellie)

that he had found it necessary to go so far for a bride. 'He might have had one nearer home', she said tartly, and turned back to her dancing.

Talking it over with her advisers, Marie de Medici decided that she need not despair. The Infanta had been promised to Charles for years, but nothing had yet come of the match and the French were convinced that nothing ever would. They were right. The Infanta was not for Charles. By autumn, he was on his way home again and even before he left Spain, Buckingham was sending a secret message to the Louvre to sound out the Queen Mother as to the availability of her youngest daughter.

Needless to say, her response was encouraging, and a few weeks later, another English visitor arrived in Paris. Viscount Kensington, handsome, affable and persuasive, was shown in to see Marie that same evening, and he lost no time in explaining his mission. He had come on behalf of the Prince of Wales, to seek Princess Henrietta's hand in marriage, he said. The Queen Mother heard him with gracious condescension and then she questioned him closely. When she was convinced that he really was a wooing ambassador, authorised by King James himself, she smiled warmly and asked him if he would like to see the Princess.

This was more than he had dared hope for, so he accepted with alacrity and when Henrietta was brought into the room he was greatly impressed. 'Little Madame', he wrote in his report home that night, 'is the loveliest creature in France and the sweetest thing in nature'. In subsequent letters, he praised her

19. *Henry, Viscount Kensington,* later Earl of Holland, 'the Wooing Ambassador', by an artist of the studio of Mytens.
(National Portrait Gallery, London)

wit, her extraordinary discretion and quickness, her beautiful singing voice, her exquisite dancing and her excellent horsemanship.

There remained the question of her size, of course. King James was worried because he had heard that she was unusually small, but the Viscount hastened to reassure him. 'Her growth is very little short of her age and her wisdom infinitely beyond it', he wrote. Moreover, the French all swore that Princess Christine had been that height when she was fourteen, and she was 'now grown a tall and goodly lady'. He did not say that Henrietta was under five feet. After all, Charles himself was only five feet four. What really mattered was that she appeared healthy and well-made. She would be able to bear children.

For her part, Henrietta was eager to know all about the Prince, his country and the British way of life, and she was continually plying the Viscount and his retinue with questions. He had several agreeable gentlemen with him and she found Henry Jermyn particularly helpful. A tall, heavily-made, fair-haired young man, he was placid and obliging and she soon made friends with him in spite of the fact that she could not speak his language.

Anxious to encourage her, they all plied her with stories about Charles's good looks, his charm and the splendour of his palaces. The Viscount took to wearing a locket round his neck, containing a flattering portrait of the Prince. He did not draw attention to it, but it had the desired effect. The royal ladies stared at it, unable to conceal their curiosity, and one day Anne of Austria

21. *Louis XIII*, Henrietta's brother, with one of his favourite dogs, by Jan Van Belcamp.
(Reproduced by gracious permission of Her Majesty The Queen)

asked him if she might look at it properly. 'Certainly', said the Viscount, taking it off and handing it to her with a flourish. She opened it, studied it admiringly and then passed it round her ladies.

Henrietta was not in the room at the time, and when she heard about the miniature she was desperate to see it for herself. She could not ask outright: that would not have been proper, nor could Anne say she wanted to inspect it again. Her husband Louis might not take any interest in her, but he was absurdly jealous. He would be furious if he heard that she was poring over the image of another man.

Always resourceful, Henrietta found a solution. She knew that the Viscount was lodging in the house of one of her former ladies-in-waiting. The lady was told to borrow the locket without saying who wanted to see it, and, when she brought it to the palace, Henrietta hurried her into her private cabinet, seized the small package and unwrapped it with a trembling hand. For a long time she stood staring at the portrait, blushing deeply. The Prince was even more handsome than she had imagined, she sighed. She could hardly bear to part with the locket and, according to Viscount Kensington, a whole hour passed before she gave it back.

He was delighted. Everything was going very well indeed. The Infanta had screamed that she would rather enter a nunnery than marry Charles, but this little French princess's reaction was very different. She was obviously enthusiastic and so were the French. Like the English, they feared the growing

19

power of the Hapsburgs, who ruled both Spain and the Holy Roman Empire. It would suit them both to make an anti-Hapsburg alliance. The Spanish were furious, of course, when they heard what was going on. Their ambassador did all he could to stir up trouble and their King even offered his brother, Don Carlos, as a husband for Henrietta instead. To add to the complications, the tiresome Countess de Soissons was telling everyone how eligible her own son was. Louis had promised the Princess to him, she wailed.

Disturbed by rumours of the growing competition, the English decided that the sooner the marriage was arranged, the better it would be. Viscount Kensington had made an excellent start, but a more experienced diplomat was needed to undertake the final discussions and so James Hay, Earl of Carlisle, arrived to join the Viscount. An ugly, sophisticated, extremely wealthy Scotsman, he would negotiate the terms of the marriage contract with Louis and Cardinal Richelieu.

He went to see Henrietta too, carrying with him letters and a parcel. Both King James and his son had written, and the parcel contained another portrait of the Prince. Henrietta was so delighted that she received it with tears in her eyes. She would send her picture in exchange, she promised, and so she did. When the French ambassador in London presented it to Charles he glanced at it without a word before handing it to one of his companions. He was still pining for the Infanta. Viscount Kensington tactfully suppressed Charles's reaction to the portrait. Instead, he gave Henrietta to understand that His Highness 'fed his eyes many times with the sight and contemplation of it'. She was duly gratified.

She was longing now for the treaty to be signed, but such weighty matters were never decided quickly, and the religious difference was providing all manner of complications. The French wanted James to give concessions to the Roman Catholics in England. He felt he could not do so because he had promised his parliament that he would never rescind the laws against them. There was also the problem of the Pope, who had expressed horror at the idea of Henrietta marrying a heretic, and was refusing to grant the necessary dispensation.

Throughout the autumn of 1624, she waited impatiently. The Duke de Chevreuse, a leading French nobleman, assured her that all would be well. He had been told he was to escort her to England once everything had been arranged, and he was so confident that he was already ordering a magnificent set of clothes for himself and gathering together the 500,000 crowns worth of diamonds he would wear. Even that did not reassure the Princess. 'The lady grows melancholy when any obstacle occurs', it was reported in London, but at long last the terms were agreed. Henrietta would bring her husband a dowry of 800,000 crowns and he would settle suitable lands on her. She would have a chapel of her own in each of her residences, and her retinue would include a bishop and twenty-eight priests. When her children were born, she would be responsible for their education until they were twelve.

The treaty was signed in Paris on 10 November 1624. It was, Henrietta told Gaston, the happiest day of her life. Bonfires were lit, cannon boomed out over the city and her mother held a series of magnificent balls in the Louvre. Even Louis XIII was looking uncharacteristically cheerful. He had really managed to annoy the Spaniards as last.

The vital dispensation had still to come, but Henrietta now received a polite letter from her future husband. He had seen her in Paris, unknown to herself, he said, and he was convinced that 'the exterior of your person in no degree

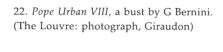

22. *Pope Urban VIII*, a bust by G Bernini.
(The Louvre: photograph, Giraudon)

belies the lustre of your virtues'. She hastened to reply, in French, of course, that if she did not really possess the good points which he imagined her to have, 'at least you will find a readiness to show you that you will not oblige an ungrateful person'. The Prince responded with a jewel worth 200,000 livres and yet another picture of himself.

Well satisfied, Henrietta began to style herself 'bride of the Prince of England, and future Queen of two kingdoms'. The Venetian ambassador noted that she was badgering her mother and her brother constantly to set a date for the wedding, but that could not be done until the dispensation came. Fuming at the delay, she was forced to wait, while Louis XIII and his mother quarrelled over the retinue she would take with her to England. According to the terms of the treaty he was supposed to name her household, but Marie would not allow that, and in the end he was forced to let her have her own way.

Christmas came and went with no word from Rome, January and February dragged slowly by and then, at the end of March, an alarming piece of news arrived from England. James I had suddenly died. He had fallen ill a few weeks before and no one had been too alarmed, but his condition had taken a turn for the worse. Henrietta's bridegroom was now King Charles I.

The French were thrown into a flurry of confusion. What would happen now? Would the marriage go through? Would he stand by the treaty or was he still hankering for the Infanta? Several days passed before word finally came that their arrangements would go ahead. Charles and Buckingham were still furious about their abortive trip to Spain. Indeed, they were now planning to make war on the Spanish and they needed this alliance with France more than ever.

By a happy coincidence, the papal dispensation arrived a few days later and with it came a special letter to Henrietta from the Pope. She must always remember, he said, that she was going into a heretical country as the champion of its oppressed Roman Catholics. He helpfully listed a series of past heroines who had done wonders in similar circumstances. Henrietta must be a second Bertha, the Frankish Princess whose marriage to the King of Kent had resulted in the conversion of England. In other words, she should try to convert Charles so that his subjects would return to their allegiance to Rome. To emphasise his message, the Pope sent her an extremely rich shrine containing relics of St Martin. She composed a suitable letter of thanks,

21

presented the shrine to her friends the Carmelites and threw herself gladly into planning the final details of her wedding.

Quarrelling courtiers were still clamouring for places in her household, her trousseau was not yet ready, and at the last minute the Archbishop of Paris had a dreadful disagreement with her godfather, the Cardinal de la Rochefoucauld. The Cardinal had been selected to perform the marriage ceremony. This was his own special right, the Archbishop stormed. He should have been chosen. When his claim was brushed aside, he retired to the country in a huff. It was hardly surprising that Henrietta felt so exhausted that she had to go to a nearby spa to recuperate.

The waters had the desired effect and she was back in Paris, fit and well, for the signing of the marriage contract on 28 April. This was a grand occasion in itself. Her ladies dressed her in a robe of cloth of gold and silver, sewn all over with gold fleurs-de-lys and encrusted with diamonds and other precious stones. Escorted by her mother and the ladies of the court, with Mademoiselle de Bourbon carrying her long train, she made her way to the King's chamber, where Louis was waiting with Gaston and all the leading members of the nobility.

When they had taken their places, the Earl of Carlisle and Viscount Kensington handed the contract to the King, and the Lord Chancellor read out its provisions. After Louis had signified his agreement, the two ambassadors went off to fetch the British King's representative. Charles would not be coming to Paris in person. He had meant to send the Duke of Buckingham as his proxy, but James I's death had upset all their arrangements. The Duke would have to stay in London to attend the old King's funeral. Instead, the Duke de Chevreuse would act on his behalf. He was French, of course, but he and Charles were both descendants of a sixteenth-century Duke de Guise and so he was an appropriate choice.

Chevreuse had been waiting in his apartments upstairs and now he appeared, clad in a magnificent black striped suit sewn all over with diamonds. He presented his letter of authority and they all signed the contract: the King, Henrietta, Marie de Medici, Anne of Austria, the Duke de Chevreuse and the two British ambassadors. When that had been done, the Cardinal de la Rochefoucauld performed the customary betrothal ceremony. Afterwards, Henrietta retired to the Carmelite convent in the Faubourg St Jacques to spend the next few days praying, resting and meditating. Her wedding would take place on 1 May.

She woke that morning to find the weather dull and grey, and before long the rain began to fall. Huge crowds had been gathering in the area outside Notre Dame since the previous evening and by midday the entire centre of the city had come to a halt. At two o'clock in the afternoon, the Princess left her apartments in the Louvre to go by coach to the Archbishop of Paris's palace close by the cathedral. However annoyed he might be, he could not refuse the use of his residence. Henrietta would dress there.

Three hours later, Louis XIII arrived and went into the palace, followed a few moments after that by his mother and his wife. A special gallery had been erected, leading from the palace entrance right down into the cathedral. Eight feet above the ground, it was supported by a series of pillars. The bases of these columns were protected by waxed cloth and the upper parts were wrapped in violet-coloured satin embroidered with gold fleurs-de-lys.

At last, at nearly six o'clock, the royal procession was ready. Led by one hundred of the King's Swiss bodyguard, drums beating and flags flying, the dignitaries began to enter the gallery. Twelve royal musicians played oboes, eight royal drummers were drumming, and then, with a rousing fanfare, the ten state trumpeters came into view. Behind them walked the solitary figure of the Grand Master of Ceremonies. After him were the Knights of the Order of the Holy Ghost in their jewel-encrusted mantles and seven heralds in crimson and gold tabards.

The Baron de Bassompierre and two other noblemen preceded the Duke de Chevreuse. He was in black once more. This was not always a mourning colour, of course. Indeed, it was a favourite with courtiers because of its dramatic effect. On this occasion, the Duke's black suit was slashed to show its gold lining and a magnificent diamond jewel flashed in his black velvet cap. Immediately behind him, the Earl of Carlisle and Viscount Kensington marched triumphantly together wearing suits of cloth of silver.

The crowds outside the gallery were jostling forward to admire all this splendour, but of course they were really waiting to see the bride herself and finally she was there, a tiny, glittering figure in a dress encrusted with gold fleurs-de-lys, a crown with a huge pendant pearl perched on her dark curls. On her right walked Louis XIII, dressed in cloth of gold and silver, and on her left was Gaston, in an equally splendid outfit. Her mother, her habitual widow's black flashing with diamonds, paced along behind her, determinedly taking precedence over Anne of Austria in her gown embroidered with gold and silver. After that came all the courtiers, including a resentful Countess de Soissons. Her son, the disappointed suitor, had been allowed to stay away, but the King had insisted that she should attend.

When the procession reached Notre Dame, they all stopped at the west door of the cathedral, where a platform had been erected under a great canopy. According to medieval tradition, a couple exchanged their vows at the door of the church before going inside for the nuptial Mass. Nearly seventy years before, Charles I's grandmother, Mary, Queen of Scots, had stood on this same spot when she married the Dauphin of France. Now Henrietta made her vows and solemnly exchanged rings with the Duke de Chevreuse. The procession then formed up again and they walked along the gallery into the cathedral. The choir was filled with members of the Paris *parlement* and civic dignitaries in their crimson, ermine-trimmed robes. The walls were hung with tapestries and cloth of gold, and special seating had been erected for the royal family beneath another magnificent canopy.

The Duke de Chevreuse escorted the bride to her place and then he retired to the Archbishop's palace with the ambassadors from Britain. As Protestants, they would not attend the Mass. On her mother's instructions, Henrietta herself did not take communion that day. She would have had to fast beforehand, and Marie de Medici was afraid that if she did so she might faint during the long service. This proved a wise precaution. The programme was already running late and the Mass lasted for two hours. It was dark by the time the bridal procession emerged from the cathedral again to walk back up the gallery to the Archbishop's palace, as cannon sounded a salute and fireworks soared into the sky.

Supper was served in the great hall of the Archbishop's palace, which had been specially decorated for the occasion with tapestries from the Louvre, and a long table reached from one end of the room to the other. The King sat at the centre, under his canopy of state, with Marie de Medici on his right and Henrietta on his left, still wearing her crown and her royal mantle. The Duke de Chevreuse was placed at her other side. The Baron de Bassompierre and

23. *James, Earl of Carlisle*, who negotiated Henrietta's marriage contract, painted in 1628 by an unknown artist.
(National Portrait Gallery, London)

24. Notre Dame Cathedral, Paris, where Henrietta was married.
(Photograph, Dr David Breeze)

25. *Claud, Duke de Chevreuse*, by an
unknown engraver.
(National Portrait Gallery, London)

26. *George, Duke of Buckingham*, in 1625,
drawn during his visit to Paris,
by Rubens.
(Graphische Sammlung, Albertina,
Vienna)

27. *Marie, Duchess de Chevreuse*, portrayed by Claude Dernet as Diana, in 1627.
(Château de Versailles: photograph, Lauros-Giraudon)

two other Marshals of France served her as each course arrived in its own procession. After the meal, the guilds of Paris paraded before her and the Swiss Guard performed an intricate marching drill. Finally, at eleven o'clock, they all retired exhausted to the Louvre. Throughout the rest of the week there were further balls and banquets, the most spectacular being the feast given by Marie de Medici in her new Luxembourg Palace. Amidst all the rejoicing, the Duke of Buckingham suddenly appeared in Paris. He had come, he said, to collect the Queen of England.

His unexpected arrival caused great excitement, not least because he was such a flamboyant figure. Well over six feet tall and majestic in bearing, he had such beautiful features that James I had thought that he resembled St Stephen. He swept into the French court, literally dripping with jewels. He had purposely ordered his tailor to sew the pearls so loosely on to one of his sumptuous suits that they were continually dropping off. When anxious servants scrambled about the floor to retrieve them, he waved them away. He was so rich he had plenty more.

The French men hated him on sight. He was unbearably arrogant, behaving as though he were a king himself. He was also far too popular with their wives. In spite of his ambiguous relationship with James I and his own happy marriage, he was known to be a compulsive womaniser and no lady seemed immune to his blandishments. Henrietta's initial reaction to him has gone unrecorded, but Anne of Austria was instantly attracted to him. Trapped in her own loveless marriage, she confided to her friends that she had found in the Duke a man she could truly love.

While the flirtatious Duchess de Chevreuse encouraged Anne's romantic languishings, Henrietta was busy with her trousseau. She was taking with her thirteen dramatic new dresses which would be sure to impress the English. Six were black, richly sewn with gold and silver, three were of cloth of silver trimmed with gold flowers, and there were dresses of red, white, green and grey satin each with its own rich embroidery, fringes and braid. The grey dress must have been particularly striking, for it had a long train and huge hanging sleeves.

For state occasions, Henrietta would wear her splendid new ermine-lined, violet velvet mantle sewn all over with gold fleurs-de-lys. Its matching dress was also scattered with French lilies. Six skirts, of blue, red, silver and buff-coloured satin were heavily embroidered in gold and silver and had matching detachable sleeves. There was a black satin riding habit and a full complement of underwear: four dozen lace-trimmed chemises, another four dozen night-chemises, a chemise so fine that it was listed separately, brassieres, caps and handkerchiefs. There were silk stockings too, gold- and silver-embroidered slippers with ribbon rosettes, and a little pair of red fur-lined boots as well as gloves of washed and perfumed leather.

Apart from the garments, she would take with her a grand selection of furnishings and personal belongings, all provided at the expense of Louis XIII. There was her great bed, for instance, with its embroidered crimson curtains, its white plumes, its layers of fancy quilts and its matching stools and chairs. Her principal Lady of Honour, Mamanga's daughter Jeanne, now the Marchioness de St George, had been given a crimson bed too, and the other ladies were supplied with beds of rather less expensive fabrics.

Henrietta's chapel plate was of silver gilt and so was her table plate, which included not only spoons, forks, plates and covered cups but an ornate *nef* or centrepiece in the shape of a ship. There was silver plate as well and table linen: napkins and tablecloths by the dozen. Her pages were provided with suits of crimson trimmed with gold and silver, and when she went out she could choose from two crimson litters, each drawn by six mules, a crimson coach with six horses in gold and silver trappings and a crimson velvet carriage for the country. Six coaches almost as splendid and three chariots had been provided for the leading members of her household, along with more than sixty horses.

Not surprisingly, it took a considerable time to gather together all this finery, not to mention the several hundred people who would take her to the coast. The Count de Tillières, former French ambassador to London, would be her Grand Chamberlain. Cardinal Richelieu's promising young relative, the Bishop de Mende, was made Grand Almoner. He would be in charge of her twenty-four priests. The Sieur de Ventelet was appointed chief usher. He and many of the others chosen had looked after Henrietta when she was a child at St Germain, and her old nurse would go along too. Others came from the Louvre: Mathurine the Fool and eleven of her mother's musicians. There were gentlemen and ladies, cooks and grooms, a surgeon, an apothecary, a tailor, an embroiderer, a perfumer, a clockmaker and a jeweller.

Apart from the retinue, all the other principal nobles were making preparations too. The Duke de Chevreuse would escort Henrietta to England, with his Duchess and their household, and the others would go as far as Boulogne to see her off. As always, they were all squabbling jealously about who should ride where in the procession, and an alarmingly large number of the ladies were in an advanced state of pregnancy, including the Marchioness de St George and the Duchess de Chevreuse.

On 23 May, the long cavalcade rode out of Paris, Henrietta travelling in a red velvet litter drawn by two mules in crimson trappings with white plumes on their heads. Her brother the King had been suffering from quinsy before they set out, and by the time they reached Compiègne, he decided that he could go no further. They would have to go on without him. At Amiens, Marie de Medici took to her bed with a fever. While they waited for her to recover, they amused themselves as best they could, walking through the town, gossiping, and speculating about Henrietta's future life in England.

The Duke of Buckingham was with them, of course, and one evening an incident took place which made the French hate him even more. Anne of Austria decided to take a stroll in a private garden in the town. She became separated from the equerry who always accompanied her, and as she turned into one of the narrow alleyways she was suddenly accosted by Buckingham. No one ever found out exactly what took place, but he obviously made some improper suggestion, for the Queen screamed. Running hastily towards her, the equerry found her standing, pale and trembling, with the Duke at her side, glaring ferociously. Exaggerated reports immediately flew round the court and everyone was furious. How dared this impudent foreigner make advances to their Queen? The sooner he was out of the country, the better pleased they would be.

By now, Charles I was sending urgent messages to ask what had happened to delay his bride, and so Marie de Medici decided that Henrietta would have to go ahead without her. She did feel well enough to accompany her a few miles out of Amiens, and there they said farewell. Henrietta knelt on the ground before her mother to ask for her blessing. Marie embraced her and handed her the letter of advice which she and her confessor had composed.

Henrietta must honour Charles as her husband and her King, it said. 'Be

28. *Cardinal Richelieu, Louis XIII's chief* adviser, by Philippe de Champaigne. (National Gallery, London)

sweet, humble and patient to his will.' She must be careful not to become contaminated with his heretical opinions: 'You need not fear telling him boldly and openly that you would rather die than give way on even the slightest point'. She should pray each day for his conversion. His grandmother Mary, Queen of Scots, had died for the Roman Catholic faith so there was good reason to hope that he might be won back to the true religion, and with him his subjects.

Mother and daughter parted tearfully, but by the time she reached Bordeaux Henrietta was in a mood of high excitement. Waiting for her there was a group of English ladies and gentlemen who had come across the Channel to meet her. Buckingham greeted them warmly and ushered forward two richly dressed ladies and a young girl. Presenting them to Henrietta, he introduced them as his wife, his sister Susan, Countess of Denbigh and his niece Mary, Marchioness of Hamilton. He was determined to insinuate them into her household as soon as possible. Henrietta acknowledged them politely and then she turned away. She already had a full complement of her own ladies. She had no desire to have the Duke's spies in her retinue, and in any event, they were Protestants.

She was more pleased to meet the man who would act as her interpreter: Sir Tobie Matthew was pleasant, and she made an excellent impression on him. 'Upon my faith', he wrote to Buckingham's mother, 'she is a most sweet, lovely

29. *Anne of Austria*, Louis XIII's wife, by Rubens.
(Rijksmuseum, Amsterdam)

creature. Believe me, she is full of wit.' She seemed full of courage, too. 'I dare give my word for her that she is not afraid of her own shadow', he said, and as for those who had hinted that she was too immature for marriage, 'Whatever they say, believe me, she sits already upon the very skirts of womanhood'. Twenty ships were waiting to take her to England. As soon as the winds dropped, they would set sail.

30. *Mary, Marchioness of Hamilton*, Buckingham's niece, painted in 1622 by Mytens.
(In the Hamilton Collection at Lennoxlove)

# 3

## ENGLAND

*H*ENRIETTA EMBARKED next morning and her little fleet made a slow crossing in calm, warm weather. At nearly eight o'clock that evening, she set foot in England for the first time. As the ships fired off a hundred-gun salute, the Earl of Arundel stepped forward to make a speech of welcome. The King, he explained, was waiting with his court at Canterbury, some miles away. He would come to her next morning, when she had rested.

The French looked askance when they heard the news. This was not the reception they had been expecting. Clouds had gathered overhead and the rain began to fall steadily. Lord Arundel announced that Henrietta would lodge that night in Dover Castle, perched high on its chalk cliff above them, and he ushered her into a litter. Her courtiers gathered their bedraggled finery about them and set off on foot up the steep hill, complaining bitterly.

When they arrived at the top, they were even more disgusted. The magnificent flint keep reared above them, a formidable fortress built by the Normans. It was excellent for defence, no doubt, but as a royal residence it left much to be desired. No less an architect than Inigo Jones, Surveyor of the King's Works, had been making alterations to the apartments but even so they presented a gloomy and depressing appearance. While Henrietta gazed around in dismay, her chamberlain exclaimed loudly that the furnishings were not nearly fine enough for a Daughter of France. To make matters worse, although nine rooms had been set aside for Henrietta and her suite, there was accommodation for very few of her attendants. The rest would have to lodge in the town. There were not even provisions for those who would stay with her. While she ate supper and retired early to bed, the Duke de Chevreuse and the other principal French noblemen had to follow Lord Carlisle back down to Dover itself for a meal. The fact that the food was surprisingly good was small consolation.

Henrietta took breakfast next morning at about ten o'clock and just as she was finishing a group of horsemen rode into the castle courtyard. King Charles had arrived. He sent up word that he would wait while she finished her meal, but she leaped to her feet at once and hurried down to meet him. He was standing waiting, a short, slight, melancholy-looking man with dark hair and a little pointed beard. He was very different from the handsome, carefree figure Henrietta had been led to expect.

Charles had been a timid and delicate child. He had suffered from rickets, and as a result he had not walked until a London shoemaker made special reinforced boots for him. When he learned to talk, he spoke with a bad stutter. He was his father's youngest surviving child, and he had always been overshadowed by his adored elder brother, Prince Henry Frederick, and his flamboyant sister Elizabeth. Henry Frederick died of typhoid when Charles was twelve, and Elizabeth left soon afterwards to marry the Elector Palatine. Their parents had long since agreed to live apart, and so Charles grew up under the eye of his affectionate but demanding father. To the casual observer, James I might have been a pathetic figure, old before his time, tottering about with his arm round the neck of his latest favourite, cracking coarse jokes and embarrassing people with his sentimentality, but beneath the unprepossess-

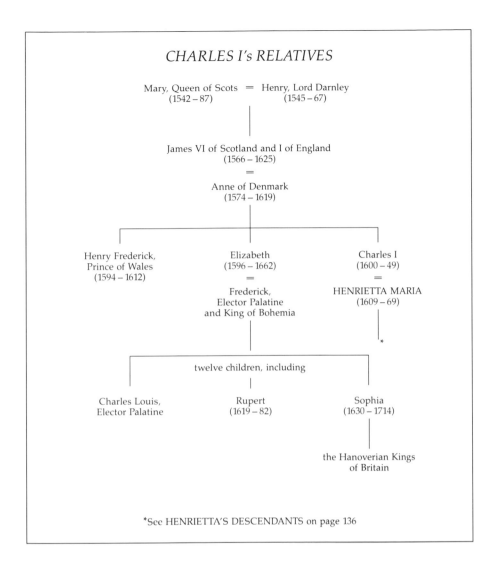

# CHARLES I's RELATIVES

Mary, Queen of Scots  =  Henry, Lord Darnley
(1542 – 87)              (1545 – 67)

James VI of Scotland and I of England
(1566 – 1625)
=
Anne of Denmark
(1574 – 1619)

Henry Frederick,          Elizabeth              Charles I
Prince of Wales           (1596 – 1662)          (1600 – 49)
(1594 – 1612)             =                      =
                          Frederick,             HENRIETTA MARIA
                          Elector Palatine       (1609 – 69)
                          and King of Bohemia
                                                            *

twelve children, including

Charles Louis,            Rupert                 Sophia
Elector Palatine          (1619 – 82)            (1630 – 1714)

the Hanoverian Kings
of Britain

*See HENRIETTA'S DESCENDANTS on page 136

ing exterior he combined a rigorous intellect with shrewd common sense. As an adolescent, Charles went in fear of him.

His situation improved dramatically with the advent of the Duke of Buckingham. At first Charles was jealous of his intimacy with the King, but that soon passed and George, eight years his senior, assumed the role of his lost elder brother. The Duke was affable, at ease with people, full of fun, everything that Charles was not. Although his speech impediment persisted, the Prince had overcome his early disability. By sheer determination he had made himself strong and athletic, a splendid horseman and a fanatical tennis-player. Under George's influence he grew in confidence and lost his nervousness of his father, but somehow, in public affairs and in his dealings with other people, he always seemed uncertain, in need of prompting.

Buckingham realised that it was to his advantage to keep Charles reliant upon him, and he became an expert at stirring up little quarrels between the

31. *Thomas, Earl of Arundel,* who greeted Henrietta at Dover, by Mytens, c.1618. (National Portrait Gallery, London)

32. Dover Castle, where Henrietta spent her first night in England. (Photograph, English Heritage)

33. *Prince Henry Frederick*, elder brother of Charles I, miniature by an artist of the studio of Isaac Oliver, painted about 1610. (National Portrait Gallery, London)

34. *Elizabeth of Bohemia*, sister of
Charles I, painted about the time of her
marriage, by an unknown artist.
(National Portrait Gallery, London)

35. *Anne of Denmark*, mother of Charles I,
by Isaac Oliver.
(National Portrait Gallery, London)

36. *James VI of Scotland
and I of England*,
Charles I's father, painted
in 1621 by Mytens.
(National Portrait Gallery,
London)

King and his son and then acting as mediator, James and Charles were then more grateful than ever to him, and with every year that passed he became more like a member of the royal family. The courtiers knew that if they wanted a pension or a title they would have to go to him. By the end of James's life, Buckingham was directing foreign policy too. The King always had the last word, of course, but the Duke's influence was enormous.

The more people hated and envied him for his power, the more solicitous did Charles become, and with James's death they drew even closer together. Their relationship was not a homosexual one: Charles would have been horrified at the very idea, but he did rely on the Duke in many ways. For his part, Buckingham knew only too well that his position was entirely dependent on the King's friendship and he viewed the advent of Henrietta with suspicion. That was why he had been so anxious to go over and inspect her for himself. Now, he watched intently as the two greeted each other for the first time.

Reaching the foot of the stairs, Henrietta knelt before her husband, trembling with excitement, and tried to kiss his hand. Before she could do so, he put his arms around her, raised her up and 'kissed her with many kisses'. She then embarked upon her carefully rehearsed speech. 'Sire,' she began, 'I have come to this country for your Majesty, to be used and commanded by you . . .' He answered her in French, and they gazed at each other searchingly. Seeing Charles glance down at her feet, she remembered that he had been worried about her height. Perhaps he thought she was wearing high-heeled shoes, even though she did reach only to his shoulder. 'Sire, I stand upon mine own feet', she said quickly, lifting the hem of her dress so that he could see. 'I have no help by art. This high am I, and neither higher nor lower.'

Touched by her ingenuousness, he led her through into the privacy of an inner apartment and there they had a long conversation which he described afterwards in one of his letters. Henrietta begged him not to be angry with her if she should make any mistakes. They would be because of her youth or her ignorance of the country's customs, she explained, and she urged him to tell her personally if she offended him in any way. She did not want him to use an intermediary. When he murmured reassurances, she was so relieved that she burst into tears.

He could see that she was thoroughly overwrought and he took her in his arms again, kissing her repeatedly and telling her humorously that he would go on doing so until she stopped crying. She had not 'fallen into the hands of strangers' as she appeared to think, he said soothingly. She was here because God had sent her to be his wife, and for his part he was 'no longer master of himself' but 'a servant to her'.

At last she dried her eyes, tidied herself and agreed to go through to where their attendants were waiting. She presented her retinue to him, in the correct order of precedence: the Bishop de Mende, the Count de Tillières, the Marchioness de St George and the others. By the time they had been introduced, dinner was ready. Charles had already eaten, but he sat down with Henrietta and began to carve pheasant and venison for her. Her confessor was at her elbow in an instant, reminding her that this was the eve of the Feast of St John the Baptist. She ought to be fasting. She should certainly not take meat. She waved him away. She knew her priorities. With a smile, she accepted the food her husband was offering, and began to eat.

When she had finished, they all went out into the courtyard. They were leaving that afternoon for Canterbury. No procession in France ever took place without everyone jostling for position and Henrietta's attendants wanted to take precedence over the English courtiers. They squabbled and tried to shoulder each other out of the way, while in the midst of the throng, the royal coach stood waiting. The King and Queen emerged and climbed aboard. At that moment, the Duke of Buckingham strode up, ushering his sister before him. He was determined that she should ride at the Queen's side. Just as he was about to hand her up into the coach, a large lady hurried forward. The Marchioness de St George, eight months pregnant, pushed rudely past Lady Denbigh and, before anyone could stop her, heaved herself up into the seat next to Henrietta.

Buckingham gave a roar of rage and the King stared at the intruder in disbelief, then ordered her sharply to get out. The Marchioness burst into a stream of protests and Henrietta joined in. Madame de St George was the Lady of Honour. This meant that she must go everywhere with the Queen, they cried. It was the custom. She always had done so. She always would.

Charles listened in icy silence. There was nothing he hated more than a scene. Hearing the commotion, the Duke de Chevreuse hastily came to the coach door. The Marchioness had no doubt taken her instructions from Marie de Medici, he said smoothly. The Queen Mother would wish the Lady of Honour to be in attendance at all times. She certainly would not expect, he added, with a baleful look at Buckingham's sister, that her daughter should ever be attended by a Protestant.

Controlling himself with difficulty, Charles gave way. Until now, he had been pleased with Henrietta. She had seemed suitably timid, submissive and eager to please. Now, looking across at her flushed face and her flashing eyes, he felt she had been transformed into another creature and he was appalled.

37. *Susan, Countess of Denbigh,* Buckingham's sister, in a painting attributed to William Larkin. (From the Collection at Parham Park, West Sussex, a house open to the public)

This incident was something he would not forget. As his wife turned her shoulder on him to chatter volubly with Madame de St George, he gave the order to move off and the coach clattered down the hill through cheering crowds.

At Barham, they found a group of English courtiers waiting for them and Henrietta was presented to the ladies on a large bowling green. She was much more beautiful than the Infanta, said one bystander, who had been in Spain. That evening, Charles and his bride were married again in the Great Hall of St Augustine's Abbey, Canterbury, and then they attended a lavish banquet in Lord Wootton's house. When it was over, Henrietta retired to the bedchamber set aside for her use and the Duchess de Chevreuse and her ladies prepared her for the night. After an irritatingly long wait, the King finally appeared. When two of his gentlemen had helped him to undress, he told the servants to leave, then he shut and bolted the doors. Not for him the jovial ceremony of friends publicly bedding the married couple. No one was going to spy on his wedding night.

Ready at last, he lay down with his wife. Neither he nor Henrietta had any previous sexual experience and she may have had only an inaccurate idea of what to expect. However dissipated some of the French nobility might be, Marie de Medici had brought her daughters up strictly. Next morning, Charles was up at seven o'clock, looking 'very jocund'. Henrietta did not appear until

39. St Augustine's Abbey, Canterbury, where Henrietta's English marriage took place.
(Photograph, A F Kersting)

much later, and the sharp-eyed courtiers thought that she seemed 'moribund' and 'not well at ease'.

As soon as she was ready, they set off for Gravesend. The plague was raging in London and so there would be no state entry into the city. Instead, they sailed up the Thames in the royal barge. A boisterous wind was blowing, but in spite of the 'vehement showers', they kept the windows open so that they could be seen by the hundreds of people who were lining the banks. They were both dressed in green, Charles sitting in a dignified manner, Henrietta waving enthusiastically to the crowds.

By the time they approached London Bridge, the river was swarming with little boats of all kinds and there were spectators wherever they looked: at windows, on roofs, aboard lighters and barges. One vessel was so overloaded that it capsized, hurling its hundred or so occupants into the water. Luckily, no one was drowned. The guns of the Tower of London fired a deafening salute and the cheers rose to a crescendo as Charles and Henrietta stepped ashore to acknowledge the welcome until a sudden violent shower sent them hurrying for shelter.

At about five in the afternoon, their barge finally moored at the steps of Somerset House, which would be Henrietta's palace, and she was shown round. Everything seemed sadly shabby and the bed in the principal apartment was so old-fashioned that the French had never seen anything like

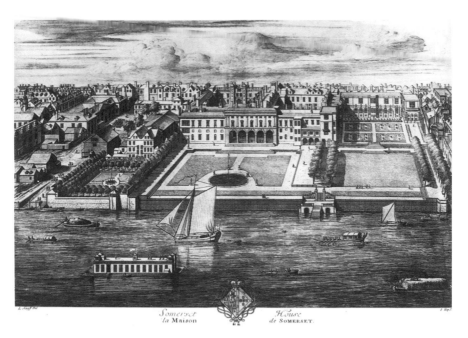

40. *Old Somerset House from the River*, Henrietta's principal residence in London, engraved by J Kip after a drawing of about 1690 by Leonard Knyff.
(Photograph, Scottish National Portrait Gallery, Reference Section Archive)

it before. Hearing their rude comments, one of the English officials explained with dignity that it had belonged to Queen Elizabeth. After that, they made their way to Charles's principal residence, the Palace of Whitehall, a rambling series of red-brick buildings, close to the river. The only modern part was Inigo Jones's magnificent stone Banqueting House.

Worn out with all the excitement, Henrietta spent her first week in London quietly, seeing no one apart from her own household. By 29 June, however,

41. *Frederick, King of Bohemia*, painted about 1630 by Gerard Honthorst.
(National Portrait Gallery, London)

42. The Chapel Royal at St James's Palace, which was refurbished by Charles I for Henrietta.
(Photograph, Royal Commission on the Historical Monuments of England)

she had recovered sufficiently to attend the formal proclamation of her marriage in the Great Hall. She and Charles sat on thrones while their marriage contract was read out to the assembled dignitaries. Afterwards, the King dined in public, but the Queen retreated to her own apartments again.

She was feeling far from happy. Everything was strange and disappointing. She was missing her own family, and the English court was very different from the lively, sophisticated place depicted by Viscount Kensington and his friends in their conversations with her. Moreover, her relationship with Charles was going from bad to worse. She shrank from him at night and by day she found him cold and preoccupied. His first parliament would meet shortly and he was desperate for the members to grant him money to equip an expedition against Spain. There was also the problem of his sister. Elizabeth's husband had become King of Bohemia, but the Holy Roman Emperor had swiftly ejected him and now he and his wife were living in exile in Holland, plying Charles with requests for military assistance.

It was all very difficult. Henrietta tried to divert him with the kind of merry badinage she and Gaston had always enjoyed, but he reacted with stiff disapproval. Unused to the company of women, he had never had a young sister to tease him and treat him with affectionate disrespect. His wife seemed to him irretrievably foreign, with her temperamental changes of mood, her tantrums and her volubility. Even her name was a problem. Who had ever heard of anyone being called Henrietta? At first he decreed that she should be known as 'Queen Henry', but no one liked that and he changed his mind and

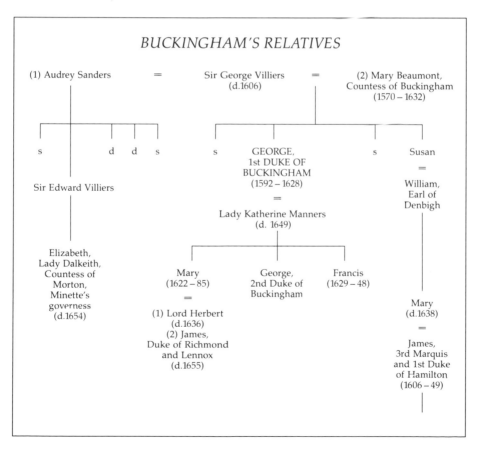

## BUCKINGHAM'S RELATIVES

(1) Audrey Sanders = Sir George Villiers (d.1606) = (2) Mary Beaumont, Countess of Buckingham (1570 – 1632)

s   d   d   s   s   GEORGE, 1st DUKE OF BUCKINGHAM (1592 – 1628)   s   Susan

Sir Edward Villiers

William, Earl of Denbigh

Lady Katherine Manners (d. 1649)

Elizabeth, Lady Dalkeith, Countess of Morton, Minette's governess (d.1654)

Mary (1622 – 85) = (1) Lord Herbert (d.1636) (2) James, Duke of Richmond and Lennox (d.1655)

George, 2nd Duke of Buckingham

Francis (1629 – 48)

Mary (d.1638) = James, 3rd Marquis and 1st Duke of Hamilton (1606 – 49)

said that officially she was to be known as 'Queen Mary' That was even worse. Although it remained the accepted form, it reminded all the Puritans of Mary Tudor and her reputation for persecuting Protestants.

In spite of these difficulties, he was not entirely immune to her attractions and, given time, he would have relaxed and accepted her innocent merriment for what it really was. Unfortunately, the Duke of Buckingham was always looming over them and when he noticed Charles smiling indulgently at Henrietta one day, he was immediately on the alert. He had hoped that this little fifteen-year-old could easily be brushed aside, but he could see that she was a person of character, with a mind of her own. He began to suspect that he had a dangerous rival and he acted at once. Playing on the King's long-standing hatred of 'the Monsieurs', as Charles always called the French, he roused up his wrath against these insolent foreigners, their painted wives and their flock of priests. When Charles recounted the latest example of Henrietta's tiresome behaviour, he was all sympathy, offering the advice of an old married man and deploring the unreasonableness of women.

He also made it his business to find out everything that Henrietta did and said. He paid members of her household to spy on her: not only English attendants, but Frenchmen too, like her equerry Pierre Civet. He was then able to interpret her every remark and action in the worst possible light. Knowing Charles as he did, it was almost laughably easy to stir up trouble between the King and Queen.

The state opening of parliament provided him with an ideal opportunity. He made sure that Henrietta was given the impression that a Church of England service was central to the occasion and of course the Bishop de Mende immediately told her not to take part under any circumstances. She stayed away, the English were offended at her absence and Charles was curt about it. His temper was not improved when the House of Commons granted him only a seventh of the money he wanted. He was forced to adjourn the session altogether when the plague grew worse, and in a mood of considerable frustration he moved to the greater safety of Hampton Court.

There, the Duke of Buckingham redoubled his efforts to sow dissension. He took to calling on Henrietta, with all manner of helpful advice. Her clothes were not right, he told her. These outlandish French fashions did not look well at the English court. Her hairstyle could be more flattering. If she tried harder with her appearance, she might please her husband more. Used to the lavish praise of her own fellowcountrymen, Henrietta listened to him with angry disbelief, but she did manage to answer him without losing her temper.

When he saw that he had not shaken her, his manner grew more menacing. The King would not put up with her sulkiness, he said. If she did not mend her ways and show him more affection, Charles would send her back to France. Unless she changed, she would no longer be treated as a Queen but as the silly little girl she was. Henrietta replied proudly that she had no intention of doing anything unworthy of a Daughter of France. If Charles had any complaint he should make it to her himself. Buckingham then demanded that she appoint his wife, his sister and his niece to her household. When she refused, he reminded her that more than one Queen of England had lost her head because she had not pleased her husband.

Soon after that, Charles set off on a hunting expedition while she went to Titchfield. His periodic visits to her were not a success and he was particularly annoyed to be told one night that she could not sleep with him because she was not feeling well. His friends the Duke of Buckingham and the Marquis of

43. *George, Duke of Buckingham*, by Mytens.
(In a private collection: photograph, Bridgeman Art Library Ltd)

Hamilton would demand their rights more frequently if she were their wife, he shouted angrily, adding, 'The little I ask of you, you make difficulties . . . I will reprimand you when you are better'. 'There is no time like the present!'

cried Henrietta, in a rage, and he stalked off and did not come to her again while she was there.

He heard about her doings, for his dear friend the Duke was quick to report any unseemly incident like the affair of the interrupted religious service. Buckingham's sister, Lady Denbigh, arranged for a Protestant to preach to the household and in the midst of the vicar's sermon the Queen and her friends suddenly appeared and marched through the congregation with their hounds, laughing, chattering and giving vent to loud hunting cries. Five minutes later they sauntered back again, with even more noise than before. Charles was so angry when he heard that he was all for sending his wife's retinue back to France, but Buckingham hastily intervened. He had not intended to endanger the alliance with Louis XIII. He persuaded the King to tolerate the foreigners for the time being, at least.

By now, the discord between Charles and Henrietta was the talk not just of London but of Paris too, and her mother and brother were far from pleased. Louis decided to send a special envoy to investigate. Confident that the Sieur de Blainville would take her part, the Queen began rehearsing a play for Christmas and paid a visit, incognito, to the Royal Exchange to do some shopping. When the Londoners recognised her they were horrified at such unconventional behaviour, and she retreated hastily to her palace again.

The Sieur de Blainville arrived early in the New Year, just in time for the next crisis. The King's coronation, postponed several times already because of the plague, was to take place at last on 2 February 1626. The English expected Henrietta to attend, and indeed the French were anxious that she too should be crowned that day. The trouble was that a Protestant Archbishop of Canterbury could not possibly be allowed to place the crown on her head. Louis consulted the learned doctors of the Sorbonne but after several weeks of debate their only suggestion was that the Bishop de Mende should crown her instead. This was totally unacceptable to the English and so when Charles went to Westminster Abbey in his white satin coronation suit, Henrietta stayed at home.

Her absence was much criticised and three days later there was another fuss. She stayed away from the opening of parliament and Buckingham stirred up a furious quarrel between Charles and herself over the choice of place from which she should watch the procession. He wanted her to go to the lodgings occupied by Buckingham's mother, she wanted to stay in her own part of the palace, and after much coming and going they ended up not speaking to each other for three days. Eventually, she requested an audience with him, asked what she had done to offend him, and although she would not apologise, begged him to forget the whole incident. He stared at her for a long time and then he smiled at her at last and took her through to his bedchamber.

With peace temporarily restored, she was able to concentrate on the rehearsals for her play. For some reason, the King had postponed the performance but it finally took place on 21 February in the hall of Somerset House. Charles and the invited audience of courtiers went along, not knowing quite what to expect, but they sat entranced as an artifical moon rose through high clouds, a storm of thunder and lightning broke and the story of innocent, courtly love unfolded. Inigo Jones had provided wonderful moving scenery, Henrietta's ladies were clad in exquisite costumes, and the Queen herself, wearing a beautiful green gown embroidered with gold, silver and pearls, took their breath away by acting the principal part. She had learned six hundred lines of French poetry for the occasion.

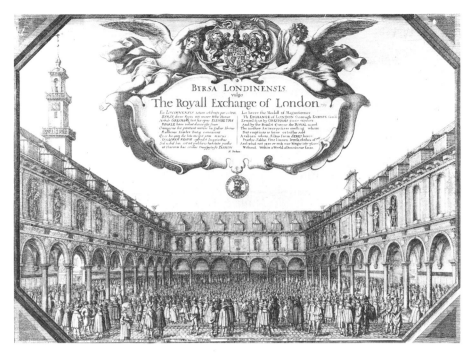

44. *The Royal Exchange*, where Henrietta went shopping: engraved by W Hollar in 1644. (Museum of London)

They all thoroughly enjoyed the evening, the King included, but the English Puritans were swift to condemn. No woman should ever appear on the stage, least of all the Queen, they protested, and to make matters worse some of her ladies had actually disguised themselves as men, with false beards. It was all Henrietta's fault, they said, and she grew more unpopular every day. So too did the Duke of Buckingham. Parliament that spring accused him of high treason, and the King had to dissolve the session hastily in case he should be condemned.

Henrietta tactfully sympathised with the Duke. Trying though it might be, she had realised that if she wanted to establish a reasonable relationship with her husband, she would have to accept the favourite and tolerate what was almost a strange ménage à trois. Charles might come to her bed at night, but Buckingham received all his confidences and provided him with the emotional support he seemed so desperately to require. Painfully, she learned to be diplomatic, and tried as best she could to foresee difficulties and counteract the Duke's continued troublemaking.

It was no simple matter, nor was her task made any easier by the fact that her husband was harassed by the attack on Buckingham and more short-tempered than ever. There were few opportunities to speak to him alone, and when she tried one night to discuss the officials who would administer her jointure lands, she found she had chosen the wrong occasion. Tired after a worrying day, Charles had just been on the verge of dropping off to sleep when she asked him to look at a list of names. He told her irritably that he would read it in the morning, but she persisted and in the end he sat up and took it from her.

These were the people she wished to undertake the work, she said. 'What!' he exclaimed immediately, 'You speak of the officials of your lands? I want you to know that you appoint no one! That is for me to do!' He was furious because

45. *Charles I* in 1628, by Honthorst.
(National Portrait Gallery, London)

she had included the names of Frenchmen. She replied briskly that his mother had always appointed her own officials, and a Daughter of France was worth more than a Daughter of Denmark. 'The Queen Mother was a good woman', Charles replied repressively, 'and a Daughter of France is not such a great thing'. If that was how he felt, cried Henrietta, he could keep his lands to himself. He bade her sharply to remember to whom she spoke, but she paid no heed, as he told Buckingham afterwards, but 'fell into a passionate discourse [as to] how miserable she was' until he finally made her keep quiet and listen to his rebukes. Shortly afterwards, he forced her to accept the Duke's female relatives into her household.

The atmosphere between them was not improved when he came to her apartments one day and found her writhing about the floor. When he asked in alarm what ailed her, he was told that she had toothache. He burst out laughing at that. Toothache was a trifling complaint, he said unsympathetically, and she must not be so feeble. She was furious. Their quarrels finally reached a climax at the end of July.

Henrietta was in the habit of going for a stroll with her ladies each afternoon, and one day Charles was informed that she had walked to Tyburn, stopped at the public gallows and said prayers for the souls of the Roman

Catholics who had died there. Henrietta denied doing any such thing, but whatever the truth of it, the King decided that he had had enough. The French attendants were filling his wife's head with undesirable ideas and ruining his marriage. They would have to go.

He and Buckingham arrived in her apartments one afternoon after a meeting of the Privy Council. Henrietta's ladies were, as usual, 'unreverently dancing and curvetting before her', so he told her in ominous tones that he wanted to speak to her in the next room. If he had anything to say, he could say it where they were, she answered pertly. He did not reply to that, but grimly ushered her attendants out of the chamber and bolted the door behind them.

Alone with his wife, he launched forth into a carefully rehearsed speech. Her retinue had done nothing but harm since their arrival and he had decided to send them home, he said. Henrietta stared at him aghast, burst into tears, flung herself on her knees and begged him to let her keep at least some of her friends. Recoiling, he shook his head. She must at least say farewell to them, she wailed, but he ignored that too and although she screamed and sobbed he remained apparently unmoved. He could be even more obstinate than she was herself.

Her cries by this time had brought her servants running to the courtyard below, and when she realised they were there she rushed hysterically to the window, broke some of the small panes of glass and clutched at the iron bars as if she would tear them out. Horrified, Charles seized her and dragged her away, bruising her arms and tearing her dress.

While his officials rounded up the French, Henrietta wept uncontrollably, refused to eat or sleep and scrawled frantic letters to her family in France begging them to help. Even Buckingham's sister was sorry for her. Lady Denbigh wrote to the Duke, pleading for the Queen's old nurse to be left with her. 'Brother', she said, 'if you did but see and hear her, it would grieve your heart to the soul. We have spoken with the King, but he will not hear us.'

In the end, he did allow the nurse to stay, along with Henrietta's dresser, Madame de Ventelet, the Protestant Duchess de Thours, one or two minor servants and the twelve French musicians. The others were ordered to leave at once. 'Force them away', Charles told Buckingham, 'driving them away like so many wild beasts until you have shipped them; and so the devil go with them.' Complaining bitterly, the Bishop de Mende, the Marchioness de St George and the others finally left for the coast, while Charles took Henrietta away to the quiet of Nonsuch, in Surrey.

# 4

## THE DEATH OF THE DUKE

WHEN THE French heard what had happened, they were most put out. Marie de Medici wept, Louis XIII was furious and Richelieu exclaimed in exasperation, 'We made that alliance for the purpose of marrying England to France, not to marry individuals'. All his plans would be spoiled unless Henrietta and Charles could be persuaded to settle down quietly together. He decided to send a new envoy to London to effect a reconciliation. The Marshal de Bassompierre had known Henrietta since her infancy, he was married to her Lord Chamberlain's sister and he had vast personal experience of matters of the heart. He had six thousand love letters to prove it. If anyone could sort out the royal couple's differences, he could.

He set sail from Boulogne on 2 October, arriving in London five days later. Buckingham welcomed him with such cordiality that he was instantly suspicious. He shared the general French antagonism towards the favourite. However, it was the Duke who would arrange his interview with the King and so he responded with his usual urbanity. Escorted by Buckingham and the Earl of Carlisle, Bassompierre was shown into a large hall. Charles and Henrietta sat on thrones on a platform at the far end. Ranged round them, in magnificent garments, were their courtiers. When Henrietta saw him, this familiar figure from her childhood, the tears came to her eyes but she managed not to weep. Bassompierre bowed low and presented his credentials. He began to explain his mission, but the King hastily interrupted to say that he would grant him a private audience later. Henrietta was all too likely to make a public scene if anything were said now about their marital difficulties.

Bassompierre retired, and a few days later he was duly summoned to Hampton Court, where he found the King waiting for him in a long gallery. The discussion which followed was more heated than cordial, but Buckingham calmed the King down. Charles agreed to continue their meetings and he even led the ambassador personally through a series of galleries to Henrietta's apartments. Bassompierre spent the next two months hurrying between the King's suite at Whitehall, the Queen's lodgings at Somerset House and the Duke of Buckingham's home, York House. That sumptuous mansion impressed him deeply. The Duke lived in a style to which even the sophisticated Frenchman was unaccustomed, and the more he saw of the Duke, the more he liked him. Both men of the world, they shared the same outlook on life and before long Bassompierre found himself agreeing that Henrietta really could be exceptionally difficult.

Buoyed up by the belief that he would miraculously settle everything in her favour, she stormed and raged about her husband's shortcomings and deliberately tried to pick a quarrel with the King whenever he came to her apartments. After one particularly embarrassing scene between the royal couple, Bassompierre decided that he had had enough. If the Queen did not mend her ways, he told her, he would go back to Louis XIII and say that her troubles were all of her own making.

That had a sobering effect on Henrietta. She was positively apologetic next time he went to see her and, a few days later, he was able to bring his delicate negotiations to a conclusion. Charles and his council agreed that henceforth

46. *Francis, Marshal de Bassompierre*, by an unknown artist.
(Bibliothèque Nationale, Paris)

the Queen would be allowed to have between forty and fifty French attendants, including ten priests and a bishop.

Her entire suite might not have been restored, but she felt that she had been vindicated. Moreover, the Duke suddenly began behaving in a friendly fashion towards her. Perhaps out of anxiety to maintain the alliance with Louis XIII, perhaps because he saw that she caused more trouble than ever when she was bullied, he put himself out to be pleasant to her.

When he gave a farewell dinner for Bassompierre, it included an entertainment specially designed to appeal to her. Each course of the magnificent banquet was accompanied by music, ballets and scene changes. Clouds came down from the ceiling and Henrietta gave an exclamation of delight as she recognised a familiar figure. Sitting on a throne on the highest cloud was a lady disguised as Marie de Medici. This personage leaned forward, beckoned, and a group of courtiers appeared, representing Gaston, Christine, Anne of Austria and various other personalities of the French court. It was so cleverly done that each was instantly recognisable and Henrietta was enchanted. The entertainment went on until four in the morning. Bassompierre departed some days later taking with him seventy Roman Catholics newly released from prison, and gifts worth £12,000, including a superb diamond from the Queen.

In the aftermath of his visit, Buckingham continued his ingratiating behaviour towards Henrietta. One night, at another banquet in York House, he had an enormous pie brought in and set before her. As she watched, intrigued, the pastry burst open and out sprang a boy, perfect in every way but only eighteen inches tall. Jeffrey Hudson the dwarf was the son of a Rutland butcher. Now aged nine, he had been for some years in the household of Buckingham's mother, but from that night on he became a member of Henrietta's retinue, and her faithful companion.

Her relationship with the Duke was helped by the fact that she was by now on much better terms with his female relatives. In the beginning, she had regarded them as spies, deliberately placed there to supplant the Marchioness de St George and her other ladies. Circumstances forced her to accept them, and as she got to know them, her natural friendliness reasserted itself. She had always liked the Duke's mother, a Roman Catholic lady of good sense, and his sister had been very kind to her when she was so upset about the retinue being sent away. Lady Denbigh was a Protestant, it was true, but she was a calm, genuinely religious person and her daughter Mary was gentle and

47. Hampton Court Palace.
(Photograph, PSA Photographic Unit)

48. *Apollo and Diana*, painted by Honthorst in 1628, possibly recording one of the court masques. Buckingham, in the guise of Mercury, leads a procession of the Liberal Arts to pay homage to Charles I (Apollo) and Henrietta (Diana). The lady looking over the Queen's right shoulder is probably the Countess of Carlisle.
(Reproduced by gracious permission of Her Majesty The Queen)

49. *Henrietta Maria and Sir Jeffrey Hudson, her dwarf*, by Sir Anthony Van Dyck.
(National Gallery of Art, Washington, Samuel H. Kress Collection)

devout. Finally, there was Buckingham's wife, witty, intelligent and good company. Now that she had cast aside her original prejudices, Henrietta found that she liked them and she treated them with the warmth and concern she always accorded to the members of her household.

Because of their closeness to the Duke, they could never be her most intimate confidantes, of course. That role was reserved for the Earl of Carlisle's wife, Lucy. A bold, high-spirited beauty ten years older than herself, Lady Carlisle was always ready to think up amusing expeditions or devise high-spirited entertainments. She also encouraged the Queen to take music lessons. Henrietta bought a lute and thoroughly enjoyed learning the instrument until her teacher, Monsieur Gouttier, was arrested for trying to rape another of his pupils, Lucy's twelve-year-old daughter.

It was generally believed to be Lucy Carlisle, too, who persuaded the Queen to start using cosmetics. Henrietta was always pale, and indeed, when the Londoners had first seen her, several had commented that she looked as though she were anaemic. Now, Lucy showed her how some subtly-placed rouge could give a more healthy appearance. The Buckingham ladies, jealous of her influence, immediately accused her of leading Henrietta astray.

Petty jealousies such as these were always part of court life, and Henrietta was becoming expert at soothing the ruffled feelings of her friends and attendants. All her new qualities of tact and diplomacy were soon to be needed, for in the spring of 1627 Louis XIII's army was besieging the Huguenots at La Rochelle and Charles and Buckingham decided to send a force to help the French Protestants. Charles would not be going himself, of course, but the Duke would lead the expedition in person. Henrietta may have been pleased to think that he would be out of the country for several months, but that hardly made up for the fact that her husband was about to make war upon her brother, and to add to her discomfort, she was aware that the British regarded their French, Roman Catholic Queen as a symbol of the enemy they were going to fight.

That spring, Henrietta was careful to identify herself with her new country's interests, but everything she said or did seemed to be interpreted in an unfavourable light. One evening the Earl of Warwick invited her to dine aboard his ship, the *Neptune,* and the next day everyone was talking about her irresponsible attitude. There she had been, riding back to Somerset House, masked, as these Frenchwomen always were in public, surrounded by her priests and sporting a jaunty little beaver hat with a black feather as though she had not a care in the world. She obviously felt no guilt about the poor Huguenots her brother was persecuting.

Far from being carefree, Henrietta was weighed down by anxieties of her own. She had received word that Louis XIII was seriously ill, and although she was not overly fond of him, she was very worried. Just as he began to recover, even worse news came from Spain. Her sister Elisabeth had died in childbed. That distressed her greatly, and when Jeffrey Hudson had a nasty fall from a window in Somerset House a few days later, she was greatly upset. He was not seriously hurt, but her nerves were already on edge and it was reported that 'she took it so heavily that she attired not herself that day.'

Perhaps most depressing of all was the thought that she had been married for two years and there was still no sign of her being with child. Maybe it would help if she took the waters. Buckingham's wife told her that he had benefited after an illness from drinking at the recently discovered chalybeate spring at Wellingborough in Northamptonshire. Henrietta decided to try it.

When she arrived in the little market town she was delighted with its picturesque buildings. There was no house large enough to accommodate her and her entourage, so they camped in the fields surrounding the Red Well. No doubt her tents were suitably grand, with all the fine furnishings she always took with her on a summer progress. Certainly she enjoyed her stay. She was optimistic that the waters would have the desired effect, and she derived endless entertainment from watching the local people perform their country dances, perhaps bringing back memories of St Germain.

She spent longer at Wellingborough than she had intended, and by the end of July Charles was sending querulous messages to the Earl of Carlisle, asking when she was coming back. He was well aware how changeable women's plans were, he said sourly, but before he could arrange his own summer progress he had to know her intentions. In the end, he went to collect her, and found himself enjoying the holiday atmosphere. 'My wife and I were never better together,' he wrote to Buckingham at the end of August, 'she . . . showing herself so loving to me, by her discretion upon all occasions, that it makes us all wonder and esteem her.'

There was still no sign of a pregnancy, however, and when they arrived back in London Henrietta decided to seek assistance of a rather different kind. Everyone was talking about the uncannily accurate predictions of Lady Eleanor Davis, who had the gift of second sight. Perhaps she could look into the future and give some encouraging news. Without saying anything to Charles, who would undoubtedly disapprove, she summoned Lady Eleanor to her presence.

Wild-eyed and strange in manner, the prophetess insisted on conversing in Latin, a language Henrietta did not understand, but the Earl of Carlisle was present and he offered to translate. Coming quickly to the point, Henrietta demanded, 'When will I have a child?' Lady Eleanor's answer was rather vague. Time would be needed, she said. Lord Carlisle tactfully interpreted this as 'Soon'.

Henrietta next asked how Buckingham would fare on his expedition against the French. He would not bring back much honour, said Lady Eleanor, but he would return shortly. With a nod, Henrietta reverted to her original line of questioning. Would her first child be a son, she demanded, and would she be happy in life? Yes, said Lady Eleanor, she would have a son, and she would be happy. 'For how long?' Henrietta persisted, perhaps unwisely. 'For sixteen years', said Lady Eleanor, unnervingly specific.

At this very moment, just as the replies were becoming really interesting, the door burst open and in came the King. When he saw what was going on, he flew into a fury. How dared this wretched woman discuss his personal affairs with the Queen? He ordered Lady Eleanor to be thrown out at once, and he told her she must never again make any predictions concerning him or his family. Not only were her prophesyings an impertinent intrusion into his private life; they could be politically dangerous too. If she suggested that any difficulties lay ahead of him, his enemies would be only too eager to repeat and exaggerate her nonsense as though it were the truth.

She was certainly right in one of her predictions. The Duke of Buckingham returned the very next week and he did not bring much honour with him. Although he himself had fought bravely, his forces had been driven back, losing both men and forty of his military standards. Putting a bold face on this humiliation, he swaggered in as if nothing untoward had happened. The King, overjoyed to have him back safe and well, hastened to take the blame

50. *The Duke of Buckingham and his Family*, after a portrait of 1628 by Honthorst. His daughter Mary, later Duchess of Richmond, is on the left, and his wife Katherine holds the baby, George.
(National Portrait Gallery, London)

51. *Thomas Killigrew and ? William, Lord Crofts*, by Van Dyck. Killigrew was Page of Honour to Charles I, and his brother-in-law Crofts was Captain of the Queen's Guard.
(Reproduced by gracious permission of Her Majesty The Queen)

52. *Anne Killigrew, Mrs Kirke*, Henrietta's dresser, who was drowned in the Thames in 1641 when the Queen's barge capsized. The portrait is by Van Dyck.
(The Huntington Library, California)

himself. He should have organised the supplies better, he said. In fact, he had played his part with uncharacteristic efficiency, but he was always self-doubting and he was only too ready to claim responsibility for the fiasco.

The British people thought rather differently and their hatred of Bucking-

53. *John Tradescant the Younger*, who suceeded his father as Henrietta's gardener. This picture, painted in 1652, is attributed to Emmanuel de Critz. (National Portrait Gallery, London)

54. *Lucy, Countess of Carlisle*, Henrietta's close friend, engraved after a painting by Van Dyck. (Scottish National Portrait Gallery)

ham rose to new heights. So did their hostility towards Henrietta. When her brother and Richelieu sent the British prisoners back to her as a gift, the gesture merely served to emphasise her close connection with the enemy. Her surgeon was arrested that winter as a French spy and when Charles appeared at the christening of Buckingham's son with his hair 'all goffered and frizzled, which he never uses before', she was blamed for persuading him to adopt this unseemly foreign style.

Determined to retrieve his military reputation, Buckingham set about planning a new expedition, amidst an atmosphere of mounting tension. One June day, when he and Charles were bowling at Spring Green, a Scotsman noticed that he was wearing his hat in the royal presence. Rushing up to him, the fellow shouted, 'You must not stand with your hat on before my King!' and he snatched the offending article from Buckingham's head. At that, the Duke 'fell to kicking him', but Charles restrained him, saying 'Let him [be], George: he is either mad or a fool'.

That same day there was much more serious evidence of dangerous hostility. Dr Lambe, Buckingham's physician, was walking through the streets of London when he was attacked, stoned by a mob and beaten to death, all because of his connection with the Duke. It was only a matter of time before they turned on the favourite himself. When Lady Eleanor Davis was consulted, she replied that he would not die yet. August would be the fatal month. 'George', said the King when he heard the rumours, 'there are some that wish that thou . . . mightest . . . perish. But care not for them. We will both perish if thou dost.'

When summer came, Charles was so involved with Buckingham's naval preparations that he had little time for his wife, and she decided to go to Wellingborough again. This return visit was not really a success. Her doctors warned her that the waters had been diluted by recent heavy rain, so they would do her little good. To make matters worse, they had not been there long when she heard that Lady Carlisle had taken smallpox. She was dreadfully upset and spent an anxious few weeks sending daily for reports on her

55. *Effigy of the Duke of Buckingham on his tomb*, in Westminster Abbey.
(By courtesy of the Dean and Chapter of Westminster)

56. *Sir Dudley Carleton, later Viscount Dorchester*, who sent Henrietta news of Buckingham's death, by Michael Jansz van Miereveldt.
(National Portrait Gallery, London)

progress. Fortunately, Lucy recovered, and after a convalescence in the country she reappeared at court again with her beauty unimpaired.

There was no chance of Charles coming to Wellingborough this year. By the late summer, Buckingham's fleet was ready to sail to France so he went to Southwick, a small village seven miles from Portsmouth, with the intention of seeing the Duke off. Buckingham took lodgings in Captain Norton's house in Portsmouth High Street. On the morning of 23 August, he decided to ride over to Southwick to visit Charles. After breakfast, he strolled down to the lower hall. It was crowded with visitors: members of his retinue, army officers, local dignitaries and the usual group of men and women trying to thrust petitions into his hands. However unpopular he might be, his influence was undiminished and any seeking royal favour knew that they must approach him.

At the foot of the stairs, he paused to speak to Colonel Sir Thomas Fryer and Lord Cleveland. They did not notice a rough-looking stranger push his way through the throng until the man suddenly drew a dagger and lunged forward. Lord Cleveland, who had just turned away, heard the thump of the knife as it entered Buckingham's chest. He spun round, in time to see the Duke reel back, snatch it out and try to draw his sword. Blood gushing from the wound, from his nose and his mouth, he staggered and fell across a table. 'Traitor! Thou has killed me!' he groaned. His companions sprang forward to try to help, but it was too late. Within minutes, he died in his surgeon's arms.

The assassin, John Felton, was an army officer with a grudge. He thought Buckingham had prevented him from being promoted. Now, his act of vengeance accomplished, he made no attempt to escape. When people screamed, 'Where is the murderer? Where is the murderer?' he stepped forward and said, 'I am the man. Here I am'. The crowd would have lynched him, but Sir Dudley Carleton hustled him away. He pleaded guilty at his trial four days later, and the day after that he was hanged at Tyburn. His body was then taken to Portsmouth and hung up in chains for all to see.

Charles was at morning prayers when a distraught messenger arrived with the news. Seeing from their faces that something was seriously amiss, the chaplain stopped the service and there was a moment's terrible silence before

57. *Interior, with Charles I, Henrietta and the Earls of Pembroke,* painted after 1635 by an unknown artist. Jeffrey Hudson is the figure on the left.
(Reproduced by gracious permission of Her Majesty The Queen)

the King, with icy self-control, motioned him to continue. He would not betray his feelings in public. He took part in the rest of the service and when it was over, he walked to his chamber in stony silence, went in and locked the door. He did not come out again for two days.

Henrietta was still at Wellingborough. Sir Dudley Carleton wrote to her there and if, as most people believed, she felt triumphant, she gave no sign. Instead, her first, shocked thoughts were for the ladies of Buckingham's family who were her attendants. She had been too young to know what was happening the day her father had died by an assassin's knife, but she had often heard her mother speak of the horror of it. Now she hurried to them to give what consolation she could, and during the next few days everyone was impressed with her concern and her genuine kindness.

She had already told her attendants to pack up her belongings and make ready to leave. She must go to the King as quickly as possible, for she knew how greatly he must be affected by the tragedy. As soon as everyone was ready, she set out for Southwick. Charles heard that she was coming, and he rode out to meet her, desperate for comfort. They were reunited at Farnham. Only with her could he let down his guard and show his desolation. She responded with remarkable understanding and an almost maternal sympathy. During the Duke's absences they had gradually been moving towards a closer relationship. Now they fell deeply in love.

The courtiers watched with amazed disbelief. 'Every day', said the Venetian ambassador, 'she concentrates in herself the favour and love that were previously divided between herself and the Duke'. 'More true love did I never see between man and wife', said Lord Goring, and when they had recovered a little from their first surprise, the noblemen and the ambassadors decided that they approved. Henrietta was French and Roman Catholic, it was true, but she was royal and she was the King's wife. Relying upon her as he now did, he would surely not feel the need to choose a successor to Buckingham. There would be no new favourite, no arrogant, low-born upstart to deprive them all of their true position as the King's advisers.

58. *Henrietta in 1630*, engraved after a portrait by Mytens.
(Scottish National Portrait Gallery)

59. *Sir Theodore Mayerne*, court doctor to Henry IV of France, Charles I and Henrietta: an enamel miniature on gold, possibly by Jean Petitot.
(National Portrait Gallery, London)

They waited nervously to see if this new-found harmony would last, and by the end of the year they were convinced that it would. The King put on a special tournament to celebrate the Queen's birthday and took part himself, riding at the lists wearing her favour. In late November, Thomas Cary observed that the King and Queen were 'at such a degree of kindness' that one would imagine 'him a wooer again and her gladder to receive his caresses than he to make them'.

When he had to go away on state business she propped his portrait up by her bed, but even then she could not sleep, and she spent her time sighing for his return. He was back again after only four days, and her happiness was complete when she discovered early in the new year that she was pregnant at last. She sent Monsieur de Ventelet off to Paris at once to tell her mother the glad news and beg for the services of the royal midwife, Madame Peronne. When her condition was announced publicly in March, bonfires were lit, bells were rung and all the foreign ambassadors came to congratulate her. She had never been so popular since she left France.

That same month, her husband took a momentous decision. Henceforth, he would rule without parliament. The current session had produced nothing but wrangling and an insolent threat to his authority. His right to collect the tax known as tonnage and poundage had been challenged, and the Puritans were launching a bitter attack on his friend Bishop Laud's attempts to achieve uniformity of worship. They accused him of trying to introduce Roman Catholic practices into the Church of England.

The House of Commons, to Charles's mind, was obstructive and insolent. The country would be far better off without its unsettling influence. Certainly he would have no one to vote him supplies if he dissolved parliament once and for all, but with Buckingham gone he had no desire to embark on any new foreign adventure. Henrietta was urging him to end the war with France and he decided to follow her advice.

The treaty of peace between Charles and Louis was announced on Sunday 10 May 1629. The court was at Greenwich and the following day Henrietta decided to attend a *Te Deum* at her chapel in Somerset House. She travelled

60. *Mary, Duchess of Richmond*, Buckingham's daughter and Henrietta's Lady of the Bedchamber, painted about 1637 as St Agnes, by Van Dyck.
(Reproduced by gracious permission of Her Majesty The Queen)

there by water, and on the way back she was so eager to go in and tell her husband all about it that she stood up as they approached the shore. By some unhappy accident, her barge collided with the landing-stage and she was thrown backwards.

Her anxious companions hastened to help her to her feet, and to their dismay she winced, bent forward and complained of a pain. They helped her into the palace and Charles came hurrying to see her. It was nothing, she said.

The feeling was gone. During the next day or so she did have the occasional twinge and then on Wednesday of that same week the pain started again, much more violently than before. Gazing at her in concern, her horrified ladies realised that her labour had started, about ten weeks too soon.

Panic ensued. There was no midwife in the palace. Madame Peronne had not even set out yet from Paris. There was not even a doctor on hand. They sent hastily for the local midwife. They purposely did not tell her who needed her services, for they did not want news of the Queen's condition to be made public. The unsuspecting woman was taken into the palace, thinking she was to attend a servant or a courtier, but when she saw the sumptuous bedchamber and the worried attendants addressing a little lady as 'Your Majesty' she realised what was happening and she fainted clean away. There was nothing to be done but to carry her out.

Henrietta was in agony by now. The baby was not lying properly. It would be a breech birth. Charles was distraught. He sent for Dr Mayerne, his own chief physician who had once been a doctor of Henry IV of France, but before he could arrive Dr Chamberlen appeared. He had attended many different labours and he was famed for his use of a type of obstetrical forceps. The King begged him to save Henrietta at all costs. If the child died, or if the Queen could have no more children, it did not matter. Terrified that he was going to lose her, he waited and waited and at last, at about three o'clock in the morning, the doctor managed to deliver the infant, a tiny, weak boy.

While Henrietta fell into an exhausted sleep, they carried her son into the next room. They all knew there was no hope for him, and so he would have to be christened at once. The King had a sharp altercation with his wife's Grand Almoner, who was insisting that he would perform the ceremony. That was out of the question, said Charles. However brief this baby's life might be, he was the Prince of Wales, and he must be baptised into the Church of England.

Bishop Laud performed the ceremony, naming him Charles James. An hour or so later, the Prince was dead. His little body was placed in a coffin and the following evening it was carried under a black velvet canopy borne by six earls' sons to Westminster Abbey. There, before noblemen, bishops, judges, courtiers and singing-men, Henrietta's first child was buried beside his grandfather, King James.

Throughout her ordeal, the Queen had been amazingly brave. When Dr Mayerne finally arrived, he found her 'full of strength and courage'. She even remembered to send a message to France, cancelling Madame Peronne's visit, and she made a determined effort to recover her health as quickly as possible. In July she went to Tunbridge Wells to drink the waters, but she missed Charles so much that she cut short her visit and hurried back to him.

Two months later, one of her servants was running about London looking for mussels. Her Majesty had a craving for them, he explained, and everyone knew what that meant. The Queen must be pregnant again. She and Charles were both nervous after her recent experience, and so he was more attentive than ever. When the latest French ambassador, the Marquis de Châteauneuf, arrived in London he was amazed to see the King kiss the Queen 'a hundred times in an hour'. He could not help commenting. 'You do not see that in Turin', Charles replied proudly, and then, lowering his voice, he added, 'or in France!'

Marie de Medici was anxious about her daughter too. She sent across a beautiful carriage so that Henrietta would not have to walk anywhere, and an exquisite locket in the shape of a heart. 'I always wear it on my neck', said

Henrietta when she wrote back, 'for I fancy it brings me such good fortune that I am always afraid when I am without it.'

Her mother was concerned about her spiritual as well as her physical health. Old Father Philip, the Scottish priest who had become Henrietta's confessor when the retinue was sent home was not, in the Queen Mother's opinion, a suitable person for such an important office. A French bishop should be appointed instead. When the French ambassador conveyed this message, Charles commented wryly, 'Your mother is sending you a governor', to which Henrietta answered 'I am no longer a child'. Indeed, the question of the retinue did not concern her any more. As long as she had enough priests, she was happy. A new set of quarrelsome Monsieurs would simply upset her domestic peace.

The new baby was expected in May, and so a few months earlier Jeffrey Hudson and the Queen's dancing master were sent to France to fetch Madame Peronne. To everyone's horror they were captured by pirates on their way back, but the redoubtable midwife was probably equal to them, for they were released soon afterwards and they arrived in England in good time. Henrietta had intended to lie-in at Greenwich, but the plague was there and so she was forced to take up residence in St James's Palace. In a pleasant room overlooking the terrace and the deer park, she went into labour at about four o'clock in the morning on 29 May 1630. Her second child was born about noon, a big, black-haired, thriving boy. Relieved and delighted, the King rode in state to St Paul's Cathedral for a formal service of thanksgiving.

Needless to say, the Queen's priests wanted to christen the infant, but Charles sent them a message telling them not to trouble themselves about the baptism of his son as he would attend to it himself. On 27 June, Laud christened the future Charles II in a silver font presented by the Lord Mayor of London. None of the godparents could attend in person, but the Duke of Lennox stood proxy for Louis XIII, the Marquis of Hamilton represented Charles's brother-in-law the King of Bohemia, and the Duchess of Richmond took the place of Marie de Medici. Britain had a Prince of Wales at last.

# 5

## THE PERFECT MARRIAGE

*A*RRIVING BACK at Hampton Court after their summer progress together, Henrietta and Charles were delighted to find the Prince growing rapidly. Henrietta wrote to tell the Marchioness de St George, 'If my son knew how to talk, I think he would send you his compliments. He is so fat and so tall that he is taken for a year old, and he is only four months. His teeth are already beginning to come. I will send you his portrait as soon as he is a little fairer'. She did not look after him personally, of course. The baby had his own household. When he was born, Charles had chosen the Countess of Roxburghe to be his governess, but there had been an immediate outcry. She was a Roman Catholic. She would never do. He had hastily replaced her with the Protestant Lady Dorset, wife of Henrietta's Lord Chamberlain. In an attempt to mollify Lady Roxburghe, he promised her that she should have charge of the first princess to be born.

The Prince continued to thrive, and the following spring his proud mother was writing again to the Marchioness about him. 'He is so ugly that I am ashamed of him', she joked, 'but his size and fatness supply the want of beauty. I wish you could see this gentleman, for he has no ordinary manner.

61. *Charles I, Henrietta and Prince Charles*, painted in 1632 by H G Pot. (Reproduced by gracious permission of Her Majesty The Queen)

62. *Jean, Countess of Roxburghe*, Princess Mary's governess, attributed to Marcus Gheeraerts. (Grimsthorpe and Drummond Castle Trust)

63. *George, Duke of Buckingham and Lord Francis Villiers*, Buckingham's young sons, painted for Charles I in 1635 by Van Dyck. (Reproduced by gracious permission of Her Majesty The Queen)

He is so serious in all that he does that I cannot help fancying him far wiser than myself.' It was all very satisfactory, and she ended her letter, 'I must admit I am very idle, for I am ashamed to confess that I am on the increase again'.

During the next ten years she had six more children. Her first daughter, Mary, was born eighteen months after Charles. James, Duke of York followed in 1633. Elizabeth arrived two years later and then Anne, fifteen months after that. The next baby, Catherine, was stillborn, but in July 1640 there was another healthy son, Henry, Duke of Gloucester.

Just as Henrietta and her brothers and sisters had been brought up away from the court at St Germain, so her children had their nurseries at St James's Palace, a country mansion once used by Henry VIII as a hunting lodge. Lady Roxburghe came into her own as governess to Princess Mary, and the other children all had their governesses, nurses and maidservants. In addition, the Duke of Buckingham's two sons and a daughter were being brought up with the royal children. Their mother was still alive, but Charles had insisted on taking care of them, and there was also his cousin the young Duke of Lennox. The King and Queen saw their children frequently and received regular reports on them, particularly their eldest son. Not only was he Prince of Wales: he remained Henrietta's personal favourite.

She often remarked afterwards that during these years she was the happiest woman in the world, for her husband adored her. Remembering their stormy relationship at the start, the courtiers marvelled that they were now so devoted to each other, and one visiting diplomat openly expressed amazement that two such apparently incompatible people were so content together.

It was certainly true that they were very different characters, but they complemented each other perfectly. Secure at last in her husband's affection, Henrietta was able to relax and enjoy a more peaceful life than she had ever known before. Because she no longer felt the need to compete for his attention, her behaviour was less flamboyant and Charles now found endearing the very imperiousness and waywardness which had once irritated him so much. In several of their reliably reported conversations, he was obviously teasing her and enjoying her flirtatious reaction.

She had her spiritual side too, of course. No entirely skittish, superficial creature could have appealed to the deeply serious Charles. Her devotion to her Church impressed him and he admired her shrewd insights into the people around them. She did not have the knowledge to advise him on political affairs, but she was an excellent judge of character and he came to rely on her more and more, consulting her before he made any appointment to his household. The one subject they never discussed was theology. When he had signed their marriage contract he had sworn not to interfere with her religion and he observed his vow so punctiliously that he avoided the topic altogether.

Their reliance upon each other was increased by the fact that neither had any close relative near at hand. Indeed, their families were a source of worry to them rather than a means of support. Communication with the continent was always difficult, of course, but Henrietta was an inveterate letter-writer and British diplomats were continually hurrying to and fro with her hastily scrawled notes covered in blots and scored-out words. She and Christine exchanged anxious messages about their mother. Marie de Medici's protégé Cardinal Richelieu had become so powerful that she finally realised he was plotting to oust her and she asked Louis XIII to dismiss him. He refused. His wily chief minister was far more necessary to him than his overbearing mother and in the summer of 1631 she was forced to flee to the Spanish Netherlands. Her son Gaston went too.

Charles was equally ill-supplied with near relations. His only sister, Elizabeth of Bohemia, widowed now, was still living in exile in Holland, bringing up her large brood of children and nagging at him constantly to get back the Palatinate for her son. In 1635 the gloomy young Prince Charles Louis arrived in person, bringing his ebullient brother Prince Rupert with him. The

King had to explain that there was nothing he could do for them. He had no wish to be embroiled in the Thirty Years War, now raging on the continent, and he did not have the money to send any soldiers on their behalf. He did invite them to stay, of course, and during their lengthy visit he and Henrietta took them about and did their best to entertain them.

Charles shared his wife's fondness for the theatre, and they often went every week, sometimes twice, seeing Shakespeare, Beaumont and Fletcher, French comedies and Spanish tragedies. Sometimes these were put on in the playhouse at Whitehall Palace, sometime in the Phoenix Theatre in Drury Lane, and whenever they particularly enjoyed a performance, they asked for it to be repeated a few nights later. They liked Thomas Heywood's *Love's Mistress* so much that they saw it three times in the same week.

Henrietta still longed to act in plays herself and, undeterred by the criticisms levelled at her previous appearance on the stage, she commissioned Walter Montagu in 1632 to write her a lengthy pastoral, called *The Shepherd's Paradise*. Her excuse was that this would be a good way to improve her far from perfect grasp of the English language and she set to and learned her eight hundred verses with a will. Others were less enthusiastic. The Marchioness of Hamilton was heard to complain that her own part was as long as an entire play.

The performance was postponed on several occasions to allow more time for rehearsals, and when it finally took place on 9 January 1633 in the Lower Court of Somerset House, it was less than successful. Admittedly the settings were beautiful, the costumes were dazzling and everyone was impressed by the Queen's mastery of her part, but by the time the audience had sat through the seven and a half hours of complicated rhetoric they were far too exhausted to appreciate it.

There was a more sinister consequence, too. A few days after the performance, William Prynne, a leading barrister, published a virulent attack on female actors. It was obviously aimed at the Queen. He was arrested and the Court of the Star Chamber sentenced him to be fined £5000, stand in the pillory and have his ears cropped. Henrietta tried to save him from the last punishment at least, but Bishop Laud insisted on the sentence being carried out. She did not act in a play again.

Less controversially, she and Charles watched bull and bear baiting in summer and when she was not pregnant she hunted with him. Sometimes she organised her own little excursions. One spring she gathered a hundred and fifty courtiers and took them out into the country on a French-style maying expedition, to gather hawthorn. She was the first to spot a bush in flower, and she was out of her coach in a flash, breaking off a sprig and fastening it in her hat. Another time, she challenged Lord Goring to a boat race on the Thames and delightedly collected 500 crowns from him when she won.

Wherever she went, her ladies, her gentlemen, her dwarfs and her pets went too. Lord Goring was just one of a circle of admiring young gallants who kept her entertained. Their lighthearted joking and their elaborate compliments to the Queen infuriated the Puritans, but they certainly did not signify any improper behaviour on Henrietta's part. She had grown up in France at a time when courtly love was much discussed among high-born, virtuous ladies. They considered it perfectly possible to have a romantic but platonic relationship with handsome young men, and most of them remained entirely faithful to their husbands.

The thought of having an affair with another man never crossed Henrietta's mind. She loved Charles far too much even to consider it and her confessor

64. *Charles I, Henrietta and Charles, Prince of Wales, dining at Whitehall,* by G Houckgeest. (Reproduced by gracious permission of Her Majesty The Queen)

65. *Charles I and Henrietta departing for the Chase,* painted by Mytens, about 1632. (Reproduced by gracious permission of Her Majesty The Queen)

later told the Pope's special agent that she never had an immoral thought. She insisted on making her confession frequently, he said, but really she had nothing to confess. She was amazingly innocent. For their part, Henry Jermyn, Walter Montagu and her other friends would not have dared make any

66. *Charles I, Henrietta, Prince Charles and Princess Mary*, painted for Charles I by Van Dyck in 1632.
(Reproduced by gracious permission of Her Majesty The Queen)

improper advances to her. Charles might feel the occasional pang of jealousy, and there were always troublemakers ready to hint at impropriety, but one look at his wife's happy, ingenuous face was usually enough to reassure the King.

Sir Jeffrey Hudson remained one of her favourite companions, and she had other dwarfs too, like Anne Shepherd, who married Richard Gibson the miniaturist. He was only three feet ten inches tall. Their wedding was celebrated with much splendour and the King himself gave the bride away. Then, as on all other occasions, Henrietta was accompanied by some of her pets. Like her mother, she was a great animal-lover and she always had monkeys, little dogs and small birds.

Music was one of the pleasures shared by the King and Queen and their friends. Henrietta's own musicians were famous, the Frenchmen like Monsieur de la Mare, Monsieur Mari and Monsieur Duvall. She sometimes employed Englishmen too. Richard Dering, composer of motets, anthems and madrigals, had been one of the King's musicians. He entered Henrietta's household as her organist and took lodgings near her French tailor, baker and embroiderer, not far from the London Church of St Mary-in-Savoy.

Her musicians performed both sacred and secular music, now in her chapels, now in court masques, often combining with colleagues from other households. When the Inns of Court put on a masque for the King and Queen, four of the musicians of the Queen's chapel took part, forty lutes played at once and the composer was the King's musician, Henry Lawes. Charles himself was an accomplished violer and his singers and instrumentalists included members of the Ferrabosco and Lanier families who had served the English monarchy for generations.

If music was Henrietta's principal source of pleasure, Charles's first love was art. He was assembling a magnificent collection of Old Masters as well as patronising both Rubens and Van Dyck. Henrietta remembered them both from their work at the Luxembourg Palace, but while Charles commissioned Rubens to paint a magnificent allegorical ceiling for the Banqueting House at Whitehall, Henrietta was more anxious to employ Van Dyck to produce portraits of her children and herself, to send to friends. Indeed, she sat to him at least twenty-five times. As for other types of picture, she treasured devotional works but she had no interest in paintings of mythological scenes. Once, when the Pope sent her a gift of marvellous Titians and Tintorettos, Charles was beside himself with excitement but Henrietta was disappointed. It was such a pity that there were no religious subjects among them, she said sadly.

67. The interior of the Banqueting House at Whitehall, showing the ceiling painted by Rubens. (Photograph, PSA Photographic Unit)

68. *Inigo Jones*, the royal architect and designer of masques, by William Dobson.
(The Trustees of the National Maritime Museum)

Architecture appealed to her more than pictures did, and from the moment she arrived in Britain she was eager to improve her residences. As early as 1626 she was employing Inigo Jones to make her a new private chamber at Somerset House. Remodelling an existing room, he created a beautiful painted and gilded cabinet in white, gold and blue, with a marble floor and an elegant iron balcony overlooking the Thames. The French influence in its decoration was obvious. Both at Somerset House and elsewhere, the Queen was constantly involved in consultations with her architect. Much to his chagrin, she employed French designers to produce plans as well, often insisting that Inigo modify his schemes to incorporate their ideas.

Three years later he was producing a new withdrawing chamber for her at St James's, as well as creating a sculpture gallery in the garden there. An even more exciting project was also in hand. Charles's mother, Anne of Denmark, had been building a new house for herself at Greenwich, but work had stopped with her death in 1619. Now Henrietta employed Inigo to complete the charming little palace.

It was unusual in plan, consisting of two blocks, one on each side of the Deptford to Woolwich Road. Inigo built a linking bridge so that the finished house appropriately resembled the letter H in ground plan. Designed essentially for domestic living rather than formal court life, it had a handsome entrance hall in Inigo's favourite cube shape. The floor of black and white marble was laid by Italian craftsmen and the Italian artists Orazio and Artemisia Gentileschi painted the elaborate ceiling with figures and symbols representing the Arts of Peace.

The grand Tulip Staircase led up to the Queen's Bedchamber on the west side. Its beautiful ceiling was painted with French fleurs-de-lys, gods, goddesses, masks and scrolls amidst complex arabesques. On the east side, the Queen's Cabinet had another magnificent ceiling and Charles himself ordered painted panels by Rubens and Jacob Jordaens for the walls.

When the house was complete, a marble tablet was placed over the central window on the octagonal tower, bearing an inscription with the Queen's name: 'Henrica Maria Regina 1635'. In its parkland setting with extensive gardens to the north it was delightful, and much admired by everyone who came to see it. Impressed with his wife's skill, Charles bought her another residence in 1639. This was Wimbledon Palace, erected some fifty years before by Sir Thomas Cecil. Henrietta immediately began to plan extensive altera-

69. The Queen's House, Greenwich.
(Photograph, English Heritage)

70. Henrietta's bedchamber, in the Queen's House, Greenwich.
(Photograph, PSA Photographic Unit)

71. *A View of Greenwich* by A Van Stalbent and J Van Belcamp, painted about 1632, showing the half-finished Queen's House in the background, with Charles I, Henrietta and their courtiers in the foreground.
(Reproduced by gracious permission of Her Majesty The Queen)


72. *The Three Eldest Children of Charles I* (Charles, Mary and James), painted by Van Dyck, probably for Henrietta. It hung in Somerset House and was in her castle at Colombe when she died there.
(Reproduced by gracious permission of Her Majesty The Queen)

tions, employing Inigo and her French architects as usual, and bringing André Mollet across from France to lay out the gardens.

Much as she enjoyed these building projects, there was another which was even closer to her heart. Ever since her arrival in England she had longed to have a proper chapel at Somerset House and when Charles signed the treaty of peace with France in the spring of 1629 he had agreed that she should have her full complement of priests. A group of Capuchins made preparations to come over and join her household, so there was urgent need for a proper chapel.

That summer, as she lay recovering from the birth of her shortlived first son, the King promised that she should have her chapel. The site chosen was the tennis court of the palace, and she laid the foundation stone on 14 September 1629. An enormous marquee was set up for the occasion and one of the Capuchins has left a detailed description of that day. The inside of the tent had been hung with fine tapestries carried across from the palace, the floor was strewn with flowers and herbs, and an altar had been placed at the far end, ornamented with large silver-gilt candelabra and a great number of costly vessels.

Before a congregation of some 2000 people, the Queen knelt beneath a canopy of state, on a crimson velvet cushion, the French ambassador by her side. The King, of course, did not attend. Henrietta's Grand Almoner, the Abbot du Péron, celebrated High Mass, with her singers and instrumentalists providing beautiful music. The service over, the ambassador escorted the Queen to the place where the foundation stone lay waiting. It was encased in silver, and it bore an inscription recording the fact that she was performing the ceremony. She touched it reverently, and then the superintendent of the building work presented her with a special trowel, its handle covered with fine, fringed velvet. Taking mortar from a large, silver-gilt basin, she threw three trowels-full on to the stone. There were loud shouts of 'God save the Queen!' and she turned to distribute money to the workmen.

Once more, Inigo Jones had been the architect, and the chapel was one of his most important designs. As usual, Henrietta had insisted that he take into account the plans drawn up by her French architects, and endless arguments had ensued. The Capuchins sometimes suspected that he was deliberately holding up the work and only the Queen's intervention and the judicious distribution of gifts prevented an open breach between Inigo and the priests.

The final result was more than satisfactory, however. The chapel was a large, brick building. The mouldings of its eight great windows were of carved Portland stone and the doorways were faced with Purbeck marble. Externally it was plain, but the interior was breathtaking. To counter the Reformation, there were many within the Roman Catholic Church who argued that services must be made as beautiful as possible in every way to win back those who had been led astray into Protestantism. Henrietta wholeheartedly agreed with this and in conversation with the Capuchins she made it clear from the start that all who came to the chapel must find it a spiritually uplifting experience even when a service was not in progress.

Accordingly, she brought François Dieussart, a leading sculptor, to make a special structure to house the Holy Sacrament. A great arch was erected in front of the altar, with space for a choir and organ at one side and instrumentalists at the other. High above the altar was a dove, representing the Holy Ghost, and beneath it were seven layers of clouds, each inhabited by the painted figures of archangels, cherubim and seraphim, two hundred in all, some adoring the Holy Sacrament, some singing and some playing instruments. More than four hundred carefully-placed lights, as well as hundreds of tapers, created the illusion of great distances and made the figures seem twice as many as they really were. The lamp above the pyx was a red oval with rays giving the impresssion that the whole altar was ablaze.

The chapel took seven years to complete, and it was formally opened on 10 December 1636 in the presence of the Queen. When the congregation entered they found that the altar was hidden by curtains, but as soon as Henrietta was seated these were drawn back to gasps of amazement as people saw the wonders beyond. At the same moment, a concealed choir began to sing an anthem and it seemed to the astonished beholders that the angels above were actually singing and playing.

Henrietta's Grand Almoner appeared from the sacristy and mounted the steps to the altar to celebrate a pontifical High Mass sung in eight parts. The Queen wept with joy. After dinner that day she went back again to attend vespers, compline and the sermon. By then, descriptions of the chapel had flown round the capital and so many people had gathered outside that the congregation could hardly get out afterwards. Everyone wanted to see it and for three days the priests could not get the doors shut because of the crowds. Finally, on the third evening, the King gave orders that the chapel was to be cleared of visitors. He wanted to see it for himself.

Accompanied by some of his gentlemen, he stood for a long time, gazing in silence at its magnificence, and then at last he said that he had 'never seen anything more beautiful or more ingeniously designed'. When the Capuchins saw the King stand before the altar, lost in contemplation, their hopes rose. They had not come to England merely to serve the Queen. Their task was to win as many converts as possible and their great ambition was that Charles himself would convert and bring all his subjects back to Rome.

For a long time, the Pope had been disappointed at Henrietta's failure to achieve anything in that direction, but he was now given to understand that her influence over her husband was considerable. She must be encouraged to win him over. His Holiness therefore began to ply her with gifts: artificial flowers and fruit, a bottle of exotic oil, 'an extraordinary fine relic in a case' and, probably less to Henrietta's taste, 'a volume of Roman Archaeology'. He also suggested that he could appoint a special papal ambassador to her court. She was enthusiastic, and she urged Charles to agree. At first he demurred. The presence of a nuncio in England was bound to infuriate the Puritans, but on the other hand if he cooperated with Rome in this, perhaps the Pope might be able to persuade the Holy Roman Emperor to give Elizabeth of Bohemia's son his rightful lands. In the end, he agreed that the nuncio could come.

The first papal ambassador died before he could take up his appointment and instead George Con arrived, a handsome, affable Scottish priest. He came bearing more gifts for Henrietta: rosaries, a shrine of relics and a portrait of St Catherine. He had presents for her ladies too. The Queen summoned them all and Father Con handed out the gifts. There was an awkward moment when he offered his rosaries to her Protestant ladies. They accepted in some embarrassment, and to cover their confusion Sir Jeffrey Hudson shouted out with droll gestures, 'Madame! Show the father that I also am a Catholic!' At that, they all burst our laughing.

With his persuasive manner and his agreeable ways, the nuncio was soon making converts, particularly among the ladies, but Henrietta remained a disappointment to him. She refused outright to meddle in politics. She would always intercede on behalf of individual Roman Catholics, she told him, but

73. *William Laud, Archbishop of Canterbury,*
Charles I's chief adviser on ecclesiastical
affairs; painted after a portrait by Van Dyck.
(National Portrait Gallery, London)

not if it was likely to cause civil strife. She also indicated that she had no intention of trying to convert Charles. By so doing she would endanger her hard-won domestic happiness. It hurt her that she could not save his soul, but she knew that his attachment to the Church of England was as great as her allegiance to Rome.

The King had by now developed a very clear view of the universe and his own place in it. As a boy, he had studied the book of instructions his father had written for Prince Henry Frederick. James I had told his heir in no uncertain terms that the monarch is the representative of God on Earth, answerable only to Him. 'Therefore,' said James, 'You are a little GOD, to sit on his throne and rule over other men'.

Charles had thought over these writings for many months. Never one to jump to conclusions, he had to argue everything out painstakingly for himself. Indeed, he irritated Henrietta and all his officials by his seeming irresolution while he considered endlessly every aspect of a question. Once he had made up his mind, however, nothing would persuade him to change it. He was an idealist, who acted from deep inner convictions. Pondering his father's exposition of the Divine Right of Kings, he accepted the doctrine as his own.

74. *Dorothy, Viscountess Andover and her sister Elizabeth, Lady Thimbleby,* regular performers in Henrietta's masques; painted by Van Dyck.
(National Gallery, London)

By the time he was in his thirties, he had dedicated himself to the task of putting Britain in order. It was his duty, he believed, to govern both church and state. He had dissolved the English parliament and he would not summon it again. The monarch was the only source of power. All his subjects were bound by their oath of allegiance to obey him. All government flowed from him in the form of laws and the administration of justice. Former ideas about laws being made by the King in parliament were set aside. There was no place in his world for the will of the people or the representative institutions. He believed that there was no need for them. His just rule would bring harmony and benefit to everyone.

Charles did not take up this role in a spirit of self-satisfaction. The responsibilities were tremendous and he was painfully aware of his own deficiencies, but he had Henrietta as his loving and supportive partner in this challenging task. An absolute monarch shared his power with no one, not even his wife, but feeling as he did about her, he created a special place for her in his world. She was his beloved consort, theirs the ideal marriage which would set the pattern for everyone else. By their example, love would become the most powerful force in the land: not only sexual passion between husband and wife, but a pure, spiritual love between all men and women.

75. Design by Inigo Jones for
Charles I's masque costume as
Philogenes, 1640.
(The Devonshire Collections,
Chatsworth: photograph, Courtauld
Institute)

76. *Nicholas Lanier*, the famous singer and
royal musician, by Van Dyck. This painting
belonged to Charles I.
(Kunsthistorisches Museum, Vienna)

There is no doubt that these high philosophical ideas came from Charles himself. Henrietta did not have the Stuarts' fondness for intellectual debate. Of course, she was familiar with the notion of Divine Right. The kings of France believed in Divine Right too and Louis XIII and Richelieu were working hard to increase the power of the French monarchy. Accepting the concept of an absolute ruler as entirely natural and desirable, she was eager to help Charles put his plans into effect.

Politics and religion had to be left to him, of course, but he felt the need to expound his theories to his courtiers and there she could help. James I had lectured his advisers and written books. Charles had no desire to do that. In any event, many of his subjects had neither the time nor the patience to read abstruse texts. A different method was needed. With his love of the visual arts, the King decided to use court masques. In future, these expensive entertainments would not only emphasise the status of the monarch: they would have an allegorical theme and they would show people clearly what his ideal world was like.

Henrietta was full of enthusiasm. With her love of singing and dancing, she was ready to devote long hours to rehearsals. She delighted in discussing every detail of the production with Inigo Jones, for he was not only a splendid architect but a wonderful stage designer. He had travelled abroad, and he understood when she spoke of the effects she had seen in the French masques. He was responsible for the costumes too, and she always insisted that he produce several alternative designs for her, so that she could choose which she liked best.

Most winters, the King and Queen each put on a masque for the other, and they took part in both. On 9 January 1631, for instance, the King's masque was produced at the Banqueting House at Whitehall. Called *Love's Triumph*, it featured Charles as the hero and Henrietta as the Queen of Love. Taking up their favourite theme, the Queen arrived to drive out disorderliness and vice from the court of the gods, bringing back the proper virtue and honour instead.

Six weeks later, she appeared in her own masque, *Chloridia*, as a nymph who was transformed into Flora, the goddess of flowers, by the love of Zephyrus, the west wind. The subject gave ample opportunity for pretty costumes and beautiful scenery. Henrietta, the Countess of Carlisle, the Countess of Oxford and her other ladies appeared in sumptuous green dresses spangled with gold and silver and the curtain was raised instead of being pulled aside. Henrietta's masques soon became famous for such exciting novelties. In *Tempe Restor'd*, another of hers, professional women singers took the stage for the first time in Britain and the audience sat spellbound as Nicholas Lanier, Master of the King's Music, came down in a cloud to sing the leading part in a sequence representing the harmony of the spheres.

Quite possibly the courtiers were so impressed with the beauty of it all that they paid little attention to the allegorical message. However, Charles remained convinced of the masques' importance as a means of explaining his ideas and his opponents also used this method. After William Prynne's criticism of the Queen's play, the King told the Inns of Court that they must make amends for their member's treasonable conduct by putting on a new masque for Henrietta and himself.

*The Triumph of Peace* was performed in the Banqueting House at Whitehall on 3 February 1634. It cost ten times as much as any of the royal masques and it used many of the same performers. There was a difference, however. The text was distinctly critical of the King's method of ruling. Many lawyers were utterly opposed to the theory of Divine Right. The King was not entitled to make laws without parliament, they said. They dared not express these views too openly, but in this masque the figures of peace and law were seen acting together to create harmony. The message was there for all who chose to hear it. There could be no peace without law.

The text was couched in carefully diplomatic terms, of course, and the King and Queen were addressed as Jove and Themis, the parents of peace, law and justice. Listening graciously, they saw only obedience to themselves in the lavish, costly spectacle. Henrietta and her ladies joined in the dancing, Charles asked for a repeat performance later in the week and the Queen told one of the organisers afterwards that she 'never saw any masque more noble nor better performed than this was, which she took as a particular respect to herself as well as to the King her husband.'

Three weeks later, Charles presented his own masque. This time Jove, the King of the Gods, was seen reorganising heaven in imitation of the British court, and the walls of his celestial palace were carved with the word CARLOMARIA, in tribute to the royal couple's perfect marriage. Far from grasping the fact that many of their subjects were seriously dissatisfied with Charles's rule, they remained oblivious to the growing discontent around them.

# 6

## QUEEN OF THE AMAZONS

*A*FTERWARDS, HENRIETTA often used to wish that she had studied British history when she was a girl. She might then have understood what was happening, and she could have helped Charles more effectively. It was true that the problems encountered by the King had their origins deep in the past. Queen Elizabeth had managed to ignore the growing dissatisfaction with her financial and religious policies, James I had staved off an outright confrontation, and so it was left to Charles to tackle the growing storm of discontent.

He was not the man to do it. His belief in Divine Right and his longing for uniformity in church affairs aroused ever-increasing hostility and his personal diffidence and apparent inability to make up his mind rendered him incapable of taking decisive action. Giving one concession after another to his opponents, he soon lost control of the situation altogether. The Scots were in a

77. *Henrietta Maria*, by Van Dyck, about 1635.
(The Duke of Buccleuch and Queensberry, KT:
photograph, *Scotland's Story*)

78 *Marie de Medici in exile in Antwerp*, painted by Van Dyck in 1631.
(Bordeaux Musée des Beaux-Arts)

ferment over his attempts to impose a prayer book on them, the English Puritans sympathised with them and the House of Commons was openly challenging not only his fiscal policies but his determination to act without them.

To some extent, Henrietta was insulated from these troubles by her ignorance of the English Constitution and her preoccupation with her own affairs: her dancing, her masques, her children and her outings with friends. When Charles began to look drawn and careworn she was worried; when he became more and more depressed and even gave up his favourite tennis she was seriously concerned, but at that stage she had no direct involvement in what was happening.

The atmosphere at court that winter grew suddenly sombre, and the Queen's Shrovetide masque for 1638 reflected the current unease. The darkness of rebellion, evil and strife covered the earth and was not dispelled until Henrietta appeared as Queen of Light. Attended by Jeffrey Hudson, in the guise of a fairy, she drove out all dissension, but the feeling of impending doom persisted and, just three weeks later, even more alarming news came from the north. The Scottish leaders had drawn up a National Covenant, pledging themselves to defend their form of worship against what they alleged to be the King's attempts to reintroduce Roman Catholicism, and there were wild tales of people flocking to Greyfriars Church in Edinburgh to sign the document with their blood. Henrietta's friends began to talk of war.

She was very frightened. This was a dreadful threat to her cherished way of life. She had heard all about the horrors of civil war when she was a girl in France. She went to Charles one evening and pleaded with him to give the Scots whatever they wanted in order to avoid strife. Surely he could withdraw 'that fatal book' if it was the cause of the trouble. Seeing how upset she was, the King explained gently that he could not possibly give in. Religion was merely an excuse for the Scots' rebellious activities, he said, and he expounded his belief that Presbyterians were simply republicans, set on overthrowing the monarchy. Seeing his wife look more alarmed than ever, he added hastily that he could, of course, restore order any time he liked.

Somewhat relieved, Henrietta retired to her apartments and if reports of the rebels' activities made her heart sink, she was soon diverted by the arrival in England of two unexpected visitors. Her old friend the Duchess de Chevreuse had been enduring a tiresome exile in Spain after a fierce quarrel with Cardinal Richelieu. Now she had decided to call in on London. As witty and amusing as ever, she provided a welcome distraction even if Henrietta's English ladies scowled and cast jealous glances at the alluring Frenchwoman. In her first delight at seeing her again, the Queen invited her to stay on indefinitely. Somewhat to her dismay, the Duchess evinced every sign of doing just that, and so Henrietta had to pay her lavish expenses out of her own privy purse.

The other visitor was also an exile from France, and a much more ominous one at that. Marie de Medici had long since outstayed her welcome in the Low Countries and she had been sending plaintive messages for some months now, saying that she longed to see her daughter again and meet all the grandchildren. Charles was less than enthusiastic. Not only was his mother-in-law a notorious troublemaker. He feared the reaction of the Puritans to her inevitable accompaniment of Roman Catholic priests and he had the distinct suspicion that if once she came to England he would never get rid of her again.

Henrietta's feelings were more ambivalent. She knew all too well how tiresome her mother could be, but she was fond of her, sorry for her and she had been brought up to be a dutiful daughter. She felt impelled to beg Charles to let her come, and in the end he agreed. While he contemplated his mother-in-law's arrival with gloomy resignation, Henrietta exclaimed ruefully, 'Adieu, liberty!' and began preparing a luxurious suite of fifty apartments in St James's Palace. They would all be needed. Asked by one official how he would recognise the Queen Mother of France when he went to greet her, another replied, 'She brings with her six coaches, seventy horses and a hundred and sixty in her train. By this you will easily descry her'.

She landed in England in October 1638. Charles, riding out to meet her, welcomed her at Marsham in Essex. Henrietta, six months pregnant, was waiting with the children at St James's. All the leading courtiers gathered outside the palace and at the last moment Henrietta hurried down the main staircase to take her place on a chair with her sons and daughters around her.

A fanfare of trumpets heralded the arrival of the procession. As soon as she saw the royal coach, Henrietta was on her feet in an instant, running across as quickly as her condition allowed, to wrench at the door handle with trembling hands. Grooms and footmen hurried forward to help, Charles frowned in concern, and his companion, a stout figure in black, emerged. Marie de Medici was sixty-five years old now, and her once jovial face was lined and careworn. Henrietta had not seen her for thirteen years and she found her sadly changed.

Bursting into tears, she threw herself on her knees and begged for her

79. *Henrietta greeting her mother at St James's Palace*, from *Histoire de l'Entrée de la Reine Mère du Roy dans la Grande Bretagne* (1639).
(Bodleian Library, Oxford. Douce 5, Subt. 36, plate opposite sig. L1 recto)

mother's blessing. Marie de Medici wept, Henrietta wept and the royal children wept. It was just the sort of scene the King hated, all this show of emotion before the entire court. At last he managed to shepherd them indoors, his wife and her mother talking excitedly in French, the children milling around, basking in their grandmother's attention.

Installed in her refurbished apartments, Marie de Medici soon recovered her customary vigour and in no time at all she was haranguing them about her scandalous treatment at the hands of her son and the villainy of Cardinal Richelieu. She also announced that she was arranging an excellent marriage for their eldest daughter. Astonished, Charles and Henrietta asked her to explain and she described how the Prince of Orange wanted Princess Mary as a wife for his only son. Charles was affronted. Before she had even arrived in England she had been meddling in his affairs. He told her coldly that it was quite impossible. Mary was far too important to marry a mere prince's heir. When the time came, he would choose her husband himself.

Marie de Medici was annoyed but she was well used to such rebuffs and Henrietta made up for the unpleasantness by visiting her each day and by buying some of her jewels to relieve her financial difficulties. In the afternoons they often strolled in St James's Park with the children, while Charles wrestled with the Scottish problem.

By the end of December he had evolved a complicated plan for a four-pronged attack on his northern kingdom by both land and sea. Just as he was trying to work out the details, Henrietta went into labour. There were complications and for some hours she was in great danger. Her mother was at her side, and Charles, distraught, hurried between his council chamber and her room. Determined not to die, she prayed fervently to the Virgin and at last the child was born. They named her Catherine, but she died shortly afterwards.

As Henrietta lay recovering, Charles sought to distract her from her grief by consulting her about the military appointments he was making. That was a mistake. She knew nothing of the warlike capabilities of the various candidates. Always loyal to her friends, she recommended those she liked best. As a result, inexperienced men were given senior positions while others, well-qualified, were passed over. When she was better, the King explained to her that he was going to lead his army north in person.

Henrietta feared for him but, temperamentally predisposed to bold action, she was delighted that he was doing something definite at last. Eager to help

80. *The Five Eldest Children of Charles I* (Charles, Mary, James, Elizabeth and Anne), painted by Van Dyck for the King in 1637 and hung above his breakfast table at Whitehall. (Reproduced by gracious permission of Her Majesty The Queen)

and always practical, she began to think about money. This campaign would be a great drain on the overstrained royal revenues. She had no official means of raising funds, but she could ask the Roman Catholics in England to help. Innocently pleased with her good idea, she did not realise that she was playing into the hands of her enemies. The Puritans were quick to interpret her scheme as yet another attempt to increase Roman Catholic influence in Britain.

Meanwhile, Charles had ridden rapidly to York, but once there, he seemed to be doing little good. The Covenanters had raised an army of their own and had seized several important strongholds. Instead of crushing them, the King did not even meet them in battle. Hampered by his inexperienced commanders and his lack of funds, he dared not risk that. Instead, he agreed to let them hold their parliament and their general assembly, then he returned once more to London.

Henrietta was disgusted when she heard the details of what she regarded as a shameful settlement, nor was Charles happy with the situation. He felt in desperate need of a good military adviser, and so, on the recommendation of Archbishop Laud, he sent for Thomas Wentworth. A tough, energetic administrator currently in Ireland as Lord Deputy, 'Black Tom' would surely know what to do. Henrietta viewed this move with some doubt. Wentworth's manner was abrasive, he had once refused to give an Irish pension to one of her friends, and as far as she was aware, his one redeeming feature was that he had the most beautiful pair of hands she had ever seen on a man. However, Charles obviously needed him and so she resolved to tolerate him.

While the King and he spent long hours discussing Scotland, her attention

81. *Thomas Wentworth Earl of Strafford*, by an artist of the studio of Van Dyck.
(National Portrait Gallery, London)

was distracted by an accident to the Prince of Wales. Seven years old now, he broke his arm and fell seriously ill afterwards. Mercifully he recovered, but he was a very bad patient and on one occasion she even had to write him a stern note. 'Charles', she said, 'I am sorry that I must begin my first letter with chiding you, because I hear that you will not take physic. I hope it was only for this day, and that tomorrow you will do it, for if you will not, I must come to you and make you take it, for it is for your health.'

82. Henrietta's letter to Prince Charles, with her characteristic blots and signature, 'Henriette Marie R'.
(British Library, Department of Manuscripts, Harl. MS.6988, f.95)

83. Design by Inigo Jones for Henrietta's costume as Queen of the Amazons. (The Devonshire Collections, Chatsworth: photograph, Courtauld Institute)

84. *John Pym*, leader of the opposition to Charles I, seen in a woodcut after Edward Bower, 1641. (National Portrait Gallery, London)

She was busy, too, rehearsing her latest masque, although the early stages of yet another pregnancy were making her feel queasy. As usual, she played the leading part. The curtain rose to show the earth being engulfed by evil spirits. Only England was still at peace, and even it was threatened by rebellious men. While the wise, all-seeing King looked on in anguish, his subjects continued their disturbances until Henrietta came down in a cloud with a plumed helmet on her head and a sword by her side. As Queen of the Amazons, she put the troublemakers to flight and restored order to her husband's realm.

The role of the protective warrior Queen must have been very much of her own choosing. She was no longer anxious to appease the Scots. They had gone too far. The agreement Charles had made with them was humiliating and the more she heard Wentworth's opinion, the more convinced she became that he was right. He was always saying that a short, sharp campaign would put the rebels down once and for all, and this appealed to her impatient nature. Soon, they were the best of friends.

Charles, too, had begun to think that this was the answer and as a token of his trust he created Wentworth Earl of Strafford. Determined to take his advice and raise another army, he summoned the abortive Short Parliament and dissolved it again after only three weeks. Led by John Pym, a Somerset lawyer, the House of Commons had absolutely refused to give him one farthing unless he redressed their grievances. He had no intention of doing that.

While he tried to raise money by loans and by enforcing the hated Ship Money tax, apprentices rioted in the London streets, attacked Archbishop Laud's palace and screamed insults at Roman Catholics. Marie de Medici complained that she was afraid to go to sleep at night in case she was murdered in her bed, and some treacherous courtier scratched a message on a window in Whitehall Palace. 'God save the King', it read, 'God confound the Queen and all her offspring'. When Charles saw it, he smashed the glass with his own fist and persuaded Henrietta to go to the greater safety of Oatlands.

He and she were both nervous about her coming confinement, after her experiences when Catherine was born, but her fourth son arrived safely on 8 July. They named him Henry, partly for her father, partly in memory of

Charles's dead brother, but also as a compliment to herself. He would bear the title Duke of Gloucester.

A week later, the Scottish Covenanters crossed the border into England and Charles set off for the north once more. He was determined to crush the rebels this time, but after weeks of inactivity he signed yet another ignominious truce. He was forced to summon parliament once more, but instead of supporting him against the Scots, the House of Commons turned on his two leading advisers. The Earl of Strafford and Archbishop Laud were both charged with high treason and sent to the Tower of London. That done, the members went on to pass a bill designed to ensure their own continuance irrespective of the King's wishes.

Henrietta was disgusted when Charles gave the bill his consent. To agree to this 'perpetual parliament' was folly, she believed, and she lost no time in telling him so. Even though they differed over his conduct of affairs, her reproaches did not damage their relationship. Rather, their tribulations were drawing them even closer together than before. That December they were united in their grief when they lost their small daughter Anne. Just three years old, she had been suffering from fever and a cough for some months past. Her condition suddenly took a turn for the worse, and she died in her sleep one

85. *The Trial of Strafford*, engraved by W Hollar. Henrietta, marked with the letter C, sits to the left of the throne, behind Prince Charles.
(The Trustees of the British Museum)

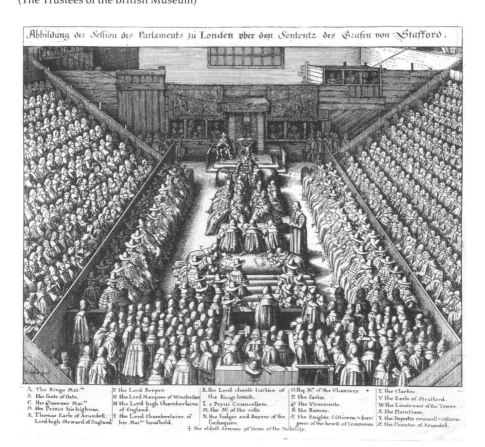

86. The interior of Westminster Hall.
(Photograph, Royal Commission on the
Historical Monuments of England)

night. Distraught, her parents called upon Dr Mayerne to perform a post-mortem, and he told them that she had been suffering from tuberculosis.

They had little enough opportunity to mourn her, for apart from all their other troubles, they now had to give serious consideration to the future of their eldest daughter. They had always intended to marry Mary to the King of Spain's heir. That would not only make a useful political alliance, but it was pleasing to Henrietta on religious grounds. Now, however, the Protestant Prince of Orange renewed his suggestion that she became his son's wife, and he offered substantial assistance in return. Henrietta was opposed to the idea, but Charles was desperate for allies and he decided to give his consent. The marriage was announced shortly before Christmas 1640.

At the end of January, Strafford appeared before the House of Lords to hear the list of charges against him. It was a long one. He was accused of misappropriating revenues, stirring up trouble with the Scots and offering to bring in the Irish army to use against the King's English opponents. Almost every day, Henrietta went with Charles to Westminster Hall to attend the trial. They sat together in a special box at one end of the hall. A screen had been erected to shield them from the public view, but Charles tore it down with his own hands so that he could smile and wave encouragement to the accused. Strafford was ill and frail, much of his vigour quenched, but as the days went by he put up an amazingly skilful defence, refuting one charge after another so effectively than even his enemies were forced to admire him.

Henrietta certainly did. Listening intently to the proceedings, she and her ladies took copious notes of what was said, in a vain attempt to find some way to help. The English legal system was not at all like the French, but the speeches were all about what the King and Strafford had said and done and so she felt well-qualified to judge the accuracy of the allegations against him. Every evening, she and Charles spoke of the evidence that day, and she longed to find some means of helping with the defence.

Nor did her efforts end there. The peers who sat in Westminster Hall and believed the lies about Strafford should be shown the truth. She resolved to win them over herself. Each night after supper, she took up a candle and crept through one of her lady's apartments and down a back stair to meet a series of muffled figures who were brought to speak to her. These were leading members of the opposition. Summoning all her eloquence, she argued, cajoled and threatened, often to no effect, but she did score one notable success with

87. *Prince William and Princess Mary*, a marriage portrait by Van Dyck. Mary wears the large diamond brooch which was William's wedding present to her. (Rijksmuseum, Amsterdam)

88. *Charles I in three Positions*, painted by Van Dyck in 1633 for the sculptor Bernini, who was to make a marble bust of the King.
(Reproduced by gracious permission of Her Majesty The Queen)

89. Medal commemorating the marriage of
Prince William and Princess Mary.
(Scottish National Portrait Gallery)

George Digby. Hitherto one of Strafford's bitterest enemies, he was suddenly converted into the Earl's staunch defender after a midnight encounter with Henrietta.

There were other mysterious goings on too: huddled groups of young noblemen caught deep in private conversation, clandestine comings and goings, suppressed excitement among the Queen's friends. At last, they revealed their plans to her. They would bring the army south, seize the Tower and release its eminent captives. Henrietta was elated. Here was real action at last. Charles, however, was not so sure. He counselled caution and when another group of conspirators revealed an almost identical plot he was soon convinced that the whole scheme was completely impractical. He would not give it his consent. Henrietta was dashed and George Goring, one of the chief conspirators, revealed both plots to Pym in a fit of pique.

At this inappropriate juncture, Princess Mary's bridegroom arrived in London for his wedding. Prince William of Orange was a well-grown, handsome lad with an amiable disposition. All too conscious of his religious shortcomings and his deplorably low rank, Henrietta ignored etiquette and refused to allow him to kiss her. Fortunately his bride was more enthusiastic. She liked him on sight and they were soon the best of friends. They were married privately in the King's Chapel at Whitehall, Mary in pearls and white satin, William in pink velvet, while Henrietta and her mother watched the Protestant service grimly through a latticed screen from a side chapel.

They all strolled amicably enough in the park that afternoon, and there were celebrations in the evening, but there was little enough cause for merriment. Strafford's trial had reached a critical point. So impressive had been his defence that Pym feared that he would be acquitted. He hastily introduced a bill of attainder which simply said that the Earl was guilty and must die. The Commons passed the bill by a majority of four to one. Hearing the news, Charles penned the Earl a reassuring note. 'Upon the word of a King', he wrote, 'you shall not suffer in life, honour and fortune.'

The bill then went to the Lords. With impeccable timing, Pym chose that moment to release the news of the Army Plots. Expressing horror and indignation, the peers passed it too, and it was sent to the King for his signature. While the conspirators fled to the continent, Strafford wrote to the King expressing his willingness to be sacrificed and Charles agonised over his terrible dilemma. Parliament was waiting for him to sign the bill, but how could he betray his old friend, the man he had promised to protect?

Outside, he could hear the screams and shouts of the crowds howling for the Earl's death and for the death of all Roman Catholics. Henrietta heard them too, and she was afraid, not least because she was told that Pym intended to separate her from Charles and imprison her for life. That was more than she could bear. She felt that she could face death bravely: after all, she was Henry IV's daughter. She could not, however, contemplate a lifelong separation from her husband.

Never one to sit and wait for disaster to strike, she rushed to Charles and begged him to flee with her to France. He apparently refused, for she sent for her coach and horses and prepared to set off for Plymouth without him. At the very moment when the coach was being driven up to the door, her Lord Chamberlain and her confessor came hurrying to see her. They pleaded with her not to leave, but she would not listen until they finally revealed the latest dreadful stories about her. People were saying that she was Henry Jermyn's mistress. He had sought refuge on the continent in the aftermath of the Army Plots. If she went too, they would say that she was on her way to join him.

Innocent, upright Henrietta was appalled. It was all very well to tolerate other people's peccadilloes. Had she not forgiven Jermyn himself when he fathered a child on one of Buckingham's nieces? For her ladies, however, and most of all for herself, she had the highest moral standards. The suggestion of a liaison with her faithful gentleman was shocking to her, and she was so upset that her Lord Chamberlain was able to lead her back to her apartments and send her coach away. She would not be going to France.

The frightening riots went on. Two nights later, her Roman Catholic servants made their confessions, expecting the mob to break in at any moment and massacre them all. Fearing for the lives of his wife and his children, Charles signed the bill of attainder. When Strafford was told, he could scarcely believe it. Until the very last, he had expected the King to save him. 'Put not your trust in princes', he exclaimed, 'nor in the sons of men, for in them there is no salvation!'

On 12 May he was taken from the Tower to his execution. As he passed the gatehouse where Laud was held prisoner, the Archbishop managed to put his hand through the bars of the window to give his old friend his final blessing, then he fell back in a faint while Strafford went bravely to his death. He was beheaded on Tower Hill before a crowd of more than a hundred thousand. Charles sat in his apartments, sunk in melancholy, and Henrietta wept inconsolably.

With Strafford gone, Henrietta became her husband's chief adviser and she watched in dismay as he gradually gave away more and more of his power. He was timid, slow and irresolute, she told one of her friends sadly. At last he decided to go to Scotland to rally support there. Determined not to stay in London at the mercy of Pym and parliament, the Queen announced that she would travel to the continent for the sake of her health. When the House of Commons discovered that she intended taking a large amount of plate and jewellery with her, they realised that she was planning to raise money for the royal cause by selling the valuables, and they told her that she could not go.

Near to despair, she wrote to her sister Christine, 'I swear to you that I am almost mad with the sudden change in my fortunes, for, from the highest degree of contentment, I have fallen into unimaginable miseries of every kind . . . Imagine my condition, seeing power taken from the King, the Catholics persecuted, the priests hung, the people who are faithful to our service sent away and indeed pursued for their lives, because they have tried

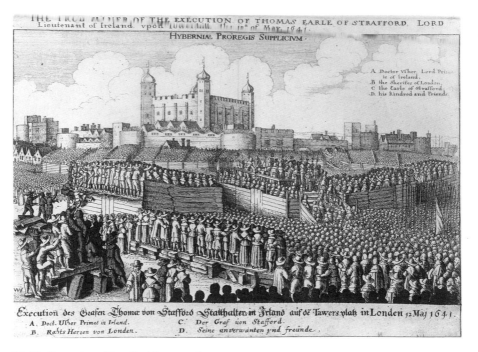

90. *The Execution of Strafford*, by an unknown engraver.
(The Trustees of the British Museum)

to serve the King, and myself kept here like a prisoner because they will not let me follow the King, who is going to Scotland, and no one in the world to whom I can confide my affliction . . .'

While Marie de Medici sought safety in the Low Countries once more, Henrietta stayed at her palace of Oatlands, trying her hardest to win the young noblemen over to her husband's cause. She was forced to live separately from her children, for parliament thought that she would contaminate them with her religious opinions, and when news of a Roman Catholic massacre of Irish Protestants reached London, public hatred of her rose to new heights. She longed for Charles to return. By all accounts he was achieving little in Scotland and in his absence parliament was drawing up a Grand Remonstrance of every imaginable grievance as well as planning to abolish the bishops.

At long last, the King came back, to a surprisingly enthusiastic welcome from the Londoners, but both he and Henrietta knew that the rejoicings were only superficial. There were sinister rumours that the House of Commons planned to impeach the Queen. For once, he did not delay. He told his Attorney General to arrest Pym, four other members of the Commons and one member of the House of Lords on a charge of treason. When he demanded that they be handed over to him, parliament refused. The King was uncertain what to do next, but Henrietta had no doubts. 'Go, you coward!' she cried, driven to distraction by his interminable vacillation, 'and pull these rogues out by the ears, or never see my face again!'

He went. Embracing her tenderly, he told her that he would be back within the hour, more powerful than he was now. He took with him five hundred soldiers and his nephew, the Elector Palatine. Henrietta waited impatiently in her cabinet, pulling out her watch every few minutes to stare at it. The time crept slowly past and just as the hour was up her door swung open. She started

91. *William Lenthall, Speaker of the* House of Commons when Charles I went to arrest the Five Members. This miniature is by Samuel Cooper, 1652.
(National Portrait Gallery, London)

up gladly, but it was only Lady Carlisle. Unable to contain her jubilation, the Queen cried, 'Rejoice! For at this very hour the King is, I hope, master in his realm and Pym, Hampden, Hazelrigg, Holles and Strode are without doubt arrested!'

She did not notice Lucy slip out a moment or two later and hurry off to her own apartments. Unknown to Henrietta, she had become the close friend of John Pym and she had been telling him everything that happened in the Queen's household. Now, she scribbled a frantic note to warn him of the danger. Even as she did so, Charles was still on his way to Westminster. He had been delayed by a crowd of people pressing round, wanting to hand him petitions. When he eventually reached the House of Commons he asked in vain for the five members. Not one of them was in his place. 'I see the birds are flown', he exclaimed curtly, and strode from the chamber.

When he arrived home, he found Henrietta in floods of tears. She told him of her dreadful indiscretion and begged him to forgive her. To her profound relief he did not utter one word of reproach. Quite probably Pym had already known, he said. This was a serious reverse, of course. The King's appearance in the House of Commons had provoked further demonstrations and he and Henrietta decided that it was no longer safe for them to stay in London. Gathering their children together, they set off in their coach through jeering crowds to Hampton Court. Nothing was ready for them there. They all had to share one bed that night, and two days later they moved to Windsor.

Charles and Henrietta were conducting all the state business themselves now, poring over papers, writing instructions, scarcely pausing to eat or sleep. They were both convinced that war was the only answer to their problems and they revived their former plan of action. Charles would go north, not to Scotland, this time, but to the northern counties of England where he believed that his subjects were still loyal to him. Henrietta would leave for the continent on the pretext of escorting Princess Mary to Holland. She did not care whether parliament gave their permission for her to leave. She was going anyhow. Nothing would persuade her to stay on in London without Charles, at the mercy of Pym and his friends.

The Dutch were relieved that their Prince's wife was coming and their ambassador Baron Van Heenvliedt hurried to court to make the necessary arrangements. He found both the King and Queen exhausted and over-wrought. During his audiences Henrietta often took the initiative, scarcely giving her husband a chance to speak, but pouring out a nervous torrent of

92. Henrietta's diamond signet with her initials and coat of arms, cut about 1628. The ring is much later than the stone.
(Reproduced by gracious permission of Her Majesty The Queen)

accusations against the rebels. On the Prince of Orange's instructions, Heenvliedt urged them to conciliate the enemy. It was far easier to get into a war than to get out of it again, he said. Charles shook his head sadly. It was no use. He had already given one concession after another, and each time the rebels had asked for more.

Heenvliedt turned to the happier subject of the forthcoming voyage. He would take the greatest possible care of Princess Mary, he said, both during the journey and afterwards. 'You have not said anything about me!' Henrietta broke in, 'I am going too, you know!' He bowed low but did not reply. He could not tell her that although the Republican Dutch were prepared to welcome the Princess, they had no desire to entertain her Roman Catholic mother. She had made up her mind to go too, and nothing would prevent her.

# 7
## HOLLAND

O N 23 FEBRUARY 1642, Henrietta, Charles and Mary went down to the shore at Dover, where a small fleet was riding at anchor in the English Channel. The Queen and her daughter would travel aboard the *Lion*, their boxes and packages were going on a special baggage vessel and the Dutch had sent Admiral Van Tromp with a squadron of fifteen ships to protect them on the voyage, for they knew that the parliamentary fleet was patrolling the North Sea, in the hope of intercepting them.

Now that the moment of parting had come, the King clung to Henrietta, murmuring endearments. They were both in tears, and she urged him over and over again not to forget his promises to her. He was to go north at once to Hull, to take charge of the store of royal munitions there, and then he was to declare war on the rebels. He should try to crush them quickly, and whatever happened he must guard against making a dishonourable peace which would in any way damage the interests of his wife and children. Knowing him as she did, she could not think how he would manage without her.

With one last reminder to him not to lose the piece of paper containing the secret code they would use in their letters to each other, she finally tore herself from his arms and marched resolutely down to the boat which was waiting to take her out to the *Lion*. Once on board, she took up her position on the deck, waving energetically to him. Desperate to keep her in view for as long as possible, he mounted his horse and rode along the pebbly shore for four leagues, brandishing his hat in a farewell salute. When his tiny figure had finally receded from sight, Henrietta dried her eyes and turned to her waiting retinue who were gazing at her dolefully.

Lord Arundel and Lord Goring were going with her. Goring had returned to the King's side soon after the betrayal of the Army Plots. Not surprisingly, Charles no longer trusted him, but Henrietta thought he could be useful. Buckingham's sister Lady Denbigh, his daughter the Duchess of Richmond and the Countess of Roxburghe, who was still Princess Mary's governess, were with the Queen, along with two of her Capuchin priests and Father Philip the confessor. As well as the usual contingent of chamberwomen, grooms, pages and footmen, there was the ubiquitous Jeffrey Hudson and the Queen's favourite dog.

Despondent at leaving their families, worried about the future and nervous of the voyage, they needed all her encouragement. The crossing was a rough one. After fifteen hours they sighted the port of Flushing but contrary winds sprang up and just as they were nearing the shore, the baggage vessel sprang a leak and sank, taking down with it not only the crew but the Queen's valuable chapel plate, most of Lord Goring's belongings and all the chamberwomen's clothing.

By the time they stepped ashore at Helvoetsluis, they were limp and exhausted. Henrietta was relieved to see Prince William waiting for them, and after a glad reunion with Mary he took them on to Brill. There, a stout, beaming, middle-aged gentleman bowed low over Henrietta's hand, with many compliments to herself and kind words for the Princess. The Prince of Orange was highly gratified at having secured such an illustrious bride for his

93. Henrietta in profile, by Van Dyck, painted about 1639 for Bernini to make a bust of her, but never sent to him.
(Reproduced by gracious permission of Her Majesty The Queen)

94. 'The New Palace', where Henrietta stayed in The Hague: bird's eye view of the Oude Hof from Blaeu's map of the city about 1640.
(Gemeente Archief, The Hague)

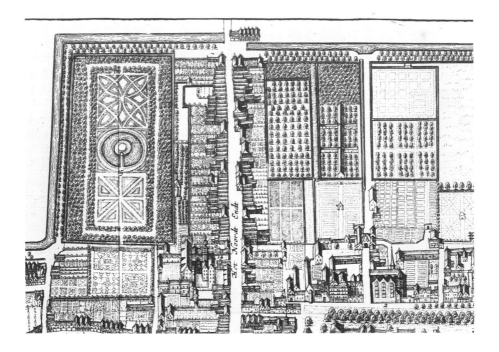

son and he ushered them joyfully into the handsome coach which would take them to The Hague. A few miles short of the capital, they saw another cavalcade coming towards them. It halted, and a large, rather untidy woman, six feet tall, emerged from the grandest vehicle and strode across to them.

Peering out of her carriage, Henrietta realised that she was about to meet Elizabeth of Bohemia for the first time. She hastily climbed out to smile and curtsey to her sister-in-law while Elizabeth towered over her and subjected her to a fierce scrutiny. She had been complaining for years that her brother paid far too much attention to his wife, and now she wanted to see the Roman Catholic Frenchwoman for herself.

Elizabeth's youngest daughter had come along too. Sharp-eyed and sharp-tongued, Sophia recorded years later in her sardonic memoirs her disappointment at seeing the Queen of England that day. Instead of the beauty from the Van Dyck portraits, she found herself staring at a thin little woman with long

95. *Mountjoy, Earl of Newport and George, Lord Goring*, both members of Henrietta's circle; after a painting by Van Dyck. (National Portrait Gallery, London)

96. *Frederick Henry, Prince of Orange*, Henrietta's helpful friend, by Miereveldt. (National Trust for Scotland, Brodick Castle)

97. *Elizabeth of Bohemia*, painted by Honthorst in 1642. (National Gallery, London)

arms and protruding teeth. However, when Henrietta told her warmly that she was even more attractive than Mary, Sophia began to think that perhaps there was something to be said for her after all.

The two Queens drove together into The Hague in a red velvet state coach to the sound of an eighty-gun salute. The Prince of Orange installed Henrietta in the handsome New Palace in the Staedt-Straat, and a few days later there was a second wedding for the young couple, celebrated with much magnificence. Henrietta could not take part, of course, because it was a Protestant service, but she kept a close eye on all the arrangements to make sure that her daughter was being treated with proper respect.

This was very necessary, because the republican Dutch seemed to have no idea how to behave towards royalty. They would wander into the room where she was seated without removing their hats, they were quite liable to sit down beside her without asking permission and some of them came up, stared at her as if she were an alien being and then walked away without uttering a word. She could not help laughing at the absurdity of it all, and she reminded Charles when she wrote to him of a similar incident in London when a Dutch envoy had bowed low over Sir Jeffrey Hudson's hand and kissed it, thinking he was the Prince of Wales.

Henrietta had little enough time for amusement, however, for no sooner was the wedding safely over then she plunged into an exhausting round of business negotiations. Summoning the local merchants, she produced an astonishing selection of jewels. There were ropes of pearls, pearl earrings, pearl bracelets, diamond finger rings and glittering gold and diamond crosses. Nor was that all. She had with her the Grand Sancy, the most valuable white diamond in Western Europe. Her father-in-law James I had bought it to wear in his hat and when Charles gave it to Henrietta she had it placed in a small crown she wore for state occasions. Now it had been taken out and put in a single setting.

Equally dazzling were two huge crucifixes. One contained the famous diamond called the Cité, and the other had at its centre an equally celebrated diamond, the Rose of England. Together, the two crosses were worth more than 200,000 livres. Another huge diamond called the Mirror of Portugal had belonged to Queen Elizabeth I, and among several ornate gold collars was one set with rubies and pearls. It had been the property of Henry VIII.

These were some of the crown jewels of England, and it was Henrietta's intention to pawn them. She had no desire to sell them outright: when the troubles were over she would want them back again, but for the time being she needed ready money, right away. She foresaw no difficulty: after all, Charles had pawned jewels in the Low Countries when he and Buckingham were financing their naval expeditions. Well-instructed by her mother from her earliest days, she knew the value of all the stones and she intended to haggle until she got the money she needed.

She was surprised and indignant when, instead of falling on the jewels with delight, the merchants shook their heads and turned away. They could not do business with her, nor could the others she sent for in the weeks that followed. Some of the large pieces, like the Henry VIII collar, were simply too expensive. No one had the kind of money needed. There was more to it than that, however. The English parliament had already sent agents across to Holland, to tell the merchants that the jewels were not the Queen's to pawn. They even put about the story that she had taken them without the King's permission.

AFBEELDING van de VISITE van Haare MAJESTEYT van GROOT BRITTANIE HENRIETTA MARIA, met haare Neef PRINS WILLEM van NASSAU, Gegeven aan den HEERE ADRIANUS PAAUW, Heere van HEEMSTEDE-OP 'T SLOT te HEEMSTEDE den agtsten September 1644.

98. *Henrietta and her son-in-law Prince William visiting Heemstede Castle,* a contemporary engraving.
(Rijksmuseum, Amsterdam)

99. *Small crown worn by Henrietta*, drawn by Thomas Cletscher.
(Museum Boymans van Beuningen, Rotterdam)

Henrietta demanded and cajoled, but she made little progress. They did agree to buy from her some of the smaller, personal items. They took her gold cross and Charles's pearl buttons. 'You cannot imagine how handsome the buttons were when they were out of the gold and strung on a chain', she wrote to him. 'I assure you that I gave them up with no small regret'. Determined to dispose of the other pieces too, she dispatched Lord Goring to try his luck with the ruby collar in Antwerp and she wrote to her husband's Danish relatives to see if they were interested in another collar.

Convinced that the diamond dealers in Amsterdam would be unable to resist the Cité and the Rose of England, she persuaded the Prince of Orange to take her there in May. She would have liked it to be a private, business trip but he insisted on proper ceremonial and they entered the city in a royal barge drawn by live swans. In a fever of impatience, Henrietta had to sit through speeches, displays and pageants before she could see the merchants and she had hardly begun her negotiations with them when one of the Prince's daughters died suddenly and they had to hurry back to The Hague.

Often reduced to tears of frustration, Henrietta was tortured by worries about what was going on in England. Communications were difficult. She had to find a reliable courier, the winds had to be in the right direction and there was always the danger that her letters would fall into the hands of the parliamentarians, who were still patrolling the North Sea. She wrote almost daily to Charles: it was her only comfort. His letters were less frequent and when they did come they were a source of torment rather than solace. Instead of following their prearranged plan to seize Hull, he seemed to be doing nothing at all. When she asked why he delayed, he replied that he was waiting for the enemy to make the first move so that everyone would see who was really to blame for his troubles.

Henrietta read his words with angry disbelief. At this rate time would go by, the money would all be spent and he still would have done nothing. When that happened, 'I shall be constrained to retire into a convent or beg alms!' she told him furiously. In the end, he did not go to Hull in person. He sent his ten-year-old son James and his nephew Charles Louis with an army. When the Mayor saw them coming, he slammed the town gates shut in the Prince's face. 'I have wished myself in James's place in Hull', said Henrietta. 'I would have flung the scoundrel over the walls before he did that to *me*.'

She did not reproach Charles too much about the loss of the Hull arsenal: there was no point in doing so. She was plunged into despair, however, by his frequent references to making a settlement with the rebels, and when he spoke of handing over control of the militia to parliament she raged, 'You are beginning again your old game of yielding everything. You ruin me in ruining yourself. I should never have quitted England, for my journey is rendered ridiculous by what you do'. If he did give up the militia, she said, she would have to go into a convent, for he would be 'no longer capable of protecting anyone, not even yourself'.

The King's replies have not survived, but a fragment of one of them reveals that he did not resent her lectures. 'The weekly dispatch is newly come, but nothing from thee', he wrote, probably in July, 'which I am sure would not be if thou would but remember how welcome thy letters are to me. Indeed, I would rather have thee chide me than be silent; but do or not do, as thou will, I am and must be, Eternally thine.'

Henrietta always found inactivity hard to bear, and that spring it seemed that all her concerns were at a stand. The Prince of Orange did his best to cheer her up. He gave her three Barbary horses, which she promptly sent to Charles, he promised her eight cannon for the King and when he went away to spend the summer with his army he invited her to bring Princess Mary to an impressive military review at a place between Gouda and Utrecht.

He also turned a blind eye to the fact that several old friends had joined her household. The Dutch had forbidden her to receive any British royalist exiles but Henry Jermyn and George Digby were among those who disguised themselves and made their way to The Hague. They proved invaluable in her

100. *Charles I and Sir Edward Walker*, his secretary, during the Civil War, by an unknown artist.
(National Portrait Gallery, London)

business dealings, because Charles had now sent word that he did not want the actual money. She was to use the funds she raised to buy arms and equipment for his army.

By day Henrietta was bargaining for muskets, cannon and pikes and by night she spent long hours labouring over her correspondence. All her letters to Charles had to be put into code and he insisted that she do it herself because he did not want anyone else knowing what they said to one another, so each word had to be carefully translated into a series of numbers. Decoding his letters was an even more trying task. 'Be careful how you write in cipher', she urged him, 'for I have been driven well nigh mad in deciphering your letter. You have added some blanks which I had not and you have not written it truly. Take good care of it, I beg you, and put nothing in it which is not in my cipher. Once again, I remind you to take care of your pocket and let not our cipher be stolen.'

Her nerves on edge, plagued by toothache and headaches so violent that she could hardly see, her eyes swollen with weeping, she felt utterly miserable. 'Pray to God for me', she begged her old friend the Marchioness de St George in a letter that May, 'for be assured that there is not a more wretched creature in this world than I, separated far from the King my Lord, from my children, out of my country and without hope of returning there except at imminent peril.'

Her sons Charles and James were with the King, but Henry and Elizabeth were in London and she wrote urging her husband to send for them. He did not, and they fell into the hands of parliament, to be kept under strict supervision in the household of the Earl of Northumberland. Henrietta was worried about them and she was anxious about her mother, too.

Marie de Medici had arrived back in the Low Countries to find that no one wanted her. In the end, Rubens came to her rescue. Long years before, he had painted the triumphant scenes of her life in her beautiful Luxembourg Palace. Now, he lent her his house in Cologne but there were rumours that she was reduced to destitution, that she was ill with heart trouble, that her attendants had deserted her and she was having to break up her furniture for firewood. Henrietta wanted to go to her, but the Dutch refused to allow her to leave their country and in July she received sad news. 'Excuse my letter being so badly written', she told Charles, 'I am troubled about the loss of the Queen my mother, who died a week ago, but I only heard the news this morning. You must put on mourning and all your suite also, and all the children. Adieu, my dearest heart, I cannot write more.'

When Baron Van Heenvliedt came to see her soon afterwards he found her 'in extremity'. She said that she was longing to go back to England, adding that she was well aware that the Dutch were anxious to see the last of her. Before she could leave, though, she needed at least 800,000 francs. According to her calculations, the diamonds, rubies and pearls still in her possession were worth half as much again. Could the merchants not be told that they must accept the gems as security?

The Baron listened patiently, then he explained yet again that no one could force the merchants to cooperate. He noticed to his dismay that she could not stop trembling as she spoke to him and she made her requests so piteously that he felt upset for several days afterwards. He urged the Prince of Orange to do something, and the Prince obligingly sent word that she could use his name whenever she liked. She could even say that the jewels belonged to him, if that would help.

It did not. The large items were still spurned by the merchants but at least she had managed to dispose of the smaller pieces and by the end of July she had purchased a consignment of cannon, powder, muskets, pikes, swords and saddles. Prince Rupert would take them to England. He set off, only to be driven back. 'The winds have been so contrary', Henrietta explained to Charles, and she could not resist adding, 'over which I have as little power as you have over the parliament, since they would not obey me when I commanded them.'

Rupert was to try again soon, but, she urged, 'He should have someone to advise him, for believe me, he is yet very young and self-willed. I have had experience of him. That is why I thought it fitting to warn you of it. He is a person capable of doing anything that he is ordered, but he is not to be trusted to take a single step of his own head'. When he went, he would be leaving her 'without a *sou*, but it matters not. I will reimburse myself as soon as I can. I had rather be in want than you . . . I will die of hunger rather than you should want'.

Before Rupert departed, she received an unexpected blow. She heard that parliament was sending an ambassador, Walter Strickland, over to Holland. She was dreadfully upset. Only the King had the right to send ambassadors. This was a deliberate attempt to flout her husband's authority. It was no use complaining to the Prince of Orange. The matter was not in his hands. Far from being an absolute ruler, he seemed to be at the mercy of the States-General, the nearest equivalent in Holland to parliament.

Desperate to prevent them from receiving the man, she wrote letters, dispatched messengers with protests and spoke to everyone who might have any influence. 'I am so weary', she told Charles that night, 'having been

101. *Johann, Baron Van Heenvliedt*, the Prince of Orange's envoy, by A Van Halen. (Rijksmuseum, Amsterdam)

102. *Prince Rupert*, attributed to Honthorst, about 1641–2. (National Portrait Gallery, London)

talking all day and been in a passion about the envoy that I am afraid my letter is no sense . . . If I do not turn mad it shall be a great miracle, but provided it be in your service, I shall be content.'

To her disgust, the States-General did receive Strickland, and to make matters worse he persuaded them to arrest one of the ships Rupert was to take with him. Yet again Henrietta sprang into action, and this time she was more successful: the ship was released. It was all very wearing. 'The Queen takes it so much to heart', said Heenvliedt sadly, 'that she is quite defeated.' At this very moment, when her morale was at its lowest, she heard rumours from England that Charles was displeased with her and had been blaming her for not sending arms and money quickly enough.

Whether he had really said any such thing is unclear. Probably some stray remark had been exaggerated or misinterpreted as was so often the way with court gossip, but Henrietta believed it and she was cut to the quick. She sat down at once and composed a long, dignified letter, detailing all that she had done since their parting at Dover. Were it not for the affection she bore him, she would have been extremely disheartened, she said, and she added, 'I am resolved to serve you in spite of all the world, that I may have this pleasure in my life, that I have spared nothing for your service and that I do my duty, although I have been extremely neglected. I do not accuse you of it, for you have been deceived as well as I'.

She had felt all along that she could not possibly return to England unless he regained all his former power. Fearing that he was about to agree to something much more humiliating, she went on, 'If there is an accommodation permit me to go to France for some time for my health, for I confess that I am not capable of undergoing what I must suffer, and perhaps there I might see you; but in case there be no accommodation let me come to you. I wish to share all your fortune and participate in your troubles as I have done in all your happiness, provided it be with honour and in your defence'.

She had to wait a month for this reply, but when it came it was gratifying. He sent the Duke of Richmond to tell her how horrified he had been to read

103. *Walter Strickland*, parliamentary envoy to Holland, painted in 1651 by P Nason. (National Portrait Gallery, London)

what she had written and he assured her that he would never dream of criticising her valiant efforts on his behalf. So kind and so solicitous was the Duke that by the time she wrote back the following day she felt almost ashamed of her previous reproaches. 'I beg your pardon if I have said anything in my letters a little passionate: it is the affection I have for you which makes me do it, and my care for your honour', she explained. Her spirits quite restored, she ended merrily, alluding to the names their enemies were giving them in London, 'I'll go pray for the Man of Sin that has married the Popish Brat of France'.

104. *Robert, Earl of Essex*, parliamentary general, engraving by unknown artist.
(The Trustees of the British Museum)

100

105. *Charles, Prince of Wales, at the Battle of Edgehill*, by William Dobson. The head in the left foreground is Medusa, often associated with the goddess of war.
(Scottish National Portrait Gallery)

For the first time in months she was feeling optimistic because Richmond had told her that the King was about to move against the rebels at last. Charles had indeed raised his standard at Nottingham on 22 August 1642 and the first brief encounter of the Civil War took place on 23 September when Prince Rupert routed a small group of parliamentarian horse at Powicke Bridge. Surely the rebels would soon be crushed and she could go back.

Throughout October, she waited impatiently for news, plying Charles with letters as usual. She knew that some of her messages were falling into enemy hands and so she amused herself by concocting elaborate statements designed to give parliament all the wrong information if they intercepted any more of her mail. It gave her particular pleasure to try to make trouble for their leader. 'I received yesterday a letter from Pym', she lied, 'by which he sends me word that he fears I am offended with him because he has not had a letter from me for a long time. I beg you tell him that is not the case and that I am as much his friend as ever.' That should embarrass 'King Pym' if it were intercepted.

In November, she finally received the news she had been longing to hear. On 23 October, Charles and his army had fought the parliamentarian Earl of Essex and his forces at Edgehill. The battle itself was inconclusive but Henrietta believed that the King had won an important victory. Charles was marching to Oxford to set up his headquarters there, and he told Henrietta that it would be safe for her to sail to Yorkshire, where the Earl of Newcastle was in command of the King's northern forces. Just when she was ready to embark, the winds changed and while the weather was still against her, Newcastle sent an urgent message telling her to wait. He had been driven from York to Durham by the enemy and he did not want her to come until he had regained the city.

Henrietta prayed for a speedy departure. 'This country is too trying to the patience of persons who, like me, scarcely have any . . .', she told Charles, adding, 'I need the air of England, or at least that in which you are, to cure me of a very severe cold I have got.' Her funds had practically all gone, and she ended one letter wryly, 'Adieu my dear heart, I am going to take my supper, and as it has cost money, I must not let it be spoiled.' The one cheering piece of news that month came from France. Cardinal Richelieu was dead. Henrietta had loathed him ever since he drove her mother out and he had never shown enthusiasm for Charles's cause. Perhaps the French would be more helpful now that he was gone.

By the time Newcastle retook York it was mid-January, the very worst time of the year for a voyage, but Henrietta was determined. She sent her coaches, more military supplies and all her goods to Scheveningen where Admiral Van Tromp was waiting with eleven warships and the *Princess Royal*. The weather was so stormy that she had to shelter in a tent until the moment of embarkation came. An enormous crowd had gathered to hasten her on her way and they watched as she emerged from her tent, thanked the Prince of Orange for all his kindness, said goodbye to his wife, embraced Elizabeth of Bohemia and kissed her own daughter Mary 'with infinite tears'. She then went on board the *Princess Royal* and lay down on her little bed. With her were the Duchess of Richmond, Lady Denbigh, Lady Roxburghe and of course Sir Jeffrey Hudson and her favourite dog.

The voyage which followed was a nightmare. A strong north-east gale was blowing and for the next nine days the little fleet was battered by the worst storm in years. Dreadfully seasick, the Queen and her ladies were unable to move from their beds. The only person still on his feet was Father Treston, one of her Capuchin priests who had been a Knight of Malta earlier in his career. He was such an excellent sailor that he was able to go about assisting Henrietta and her ladies. Convinced they were going to die, her retinue all began shouting out their confessions to Father Philip and the Capuchins, and Henrietta laughed afterwards about the unexpected secrets so openly revealed to everyone aboard. As one of her priests recorded later, 'Enmities were changed into affectionate reconciliations, those who previously hated one another embraced and all begged forgiveness of each other'.

As the *Princess Royal* tacked desperately back and forth, the sails tipping over into the sea, Henrietta suddenly remembered that no English queen had ever drowned and the thought put new heart into her. 'Comfort yourselves, my dears!' she cried. She was going to survive and so were they. After that she kept up all their spirits, laughing and joking as Father Treston tried vainly to maintain his balance as he brought them something to drink.

At one point they were only twenty hours' sailing from Newcastle, but it was impossible to go on. Two of their vessels did get through but another two foundered with all their men, Henrietta's grooms, her horses and her carriages, and the *Princess Royal* and the other ships were finally driven into Scheveningen once more. As the guns of The Hague boomed out a salute to let the townspeople know that she was back, the Prince and Princess of Orange, Elizabeth of Bohemia and Princess Mary summoned their coaches and drove out to the coast. A little fishing smack was bringing Henrietta in to land and

they were so relieved when they saw it that they all ran down the sands and waded into the sea to welcome her.

She and her attendants were a sorry sight. They had not slept or eaten since they left, they were bruised and battered and their clothes were so filthy and stiff with sea salt that they had to be cut off and burned afterwards. Too weak to walk, some of the retinue had to be carried ashore. One of the Capuchins celebrated Mass at the water's edge as soon as he disembarked, but he had to be supported by a man on either side as he did so, to prevent him from collapsing.

Henrietta herself was indomitable. One of the first things she did was to write a letter to Charles letting him know that she was safe. 'God be praised that he has still spared me to serve you', she wrote, 'but I confess that I never expected to see you again . . . The only regret I felt about dying was that this accident might encourage your enemies and discourage your friends, and this consideration I confess troubled me, for, but for your sake, life is not a thing for which I fear the loss'. Her one thought was to set off again as soon as she could: 'A storm of nine days is a very frightful thing; nevertheless, when your service is concerned, nothing frightens me'. Even she had to admit that she was exhausted, however, and she ended, 'I am so stupefied that I cannot easily write more, for I have not slept during nine nights'.

# 8
## OXFORD

*F*OR THE next fortnight Henrietta waited impatiently on the coast. Her tattered ships had to be repaired and there was a further delay when, encouraged by the English, the Dutch seized one of her vessels after searching it and finding arms in the hold. She managed to get it back again and sent the States-General a stern rebuke, declaring that the weapons were merely for her own defence during her voyage. She was well aware that parliament would capture her if they could. She would be an invaluable bargaining-counter in their dealings with the King, for everyone knew that he would agree to almost anything if she were a hostage.

To add to her irritation, her companions did not share her eagerness to set out again and, as she told Charles, 'do nothing but preach to me on the dangers I am incurring and a strange conjuction of planets which will happen when I am at sea, which has never taken place since the birth of Our Lord. I say to all this, like the almanac, "God is above all". He has already saved me from a great danger; I hope that he will not abandon me, if others should arise, since the purpose of my voyage is for a cause so just'.

At last they were ready. The weather was calm when she left Scheveningen and mercifully the voyage passed without incident. As they approached the English coast the wind veered, forcing them south to Bridlington Bay where they dropped anchor. Henrietta waited on board until a party of royalist cavalry arrived to protect her, then she landed and made her way to a thatched house near the quay. The local people came flocking to see her, bringing provisions, and as she sat down to supper William, Earl of Newcastle, arrived. He was an old friend, for he had been Prince Charles's tutor. Poet, playwright and patron of Van Dyck, he was said to be the best horseman in Europe. They had a long talk, after which Henrietta reviewed the soldiers and retired for the

107. Bridlington Bay as it is today.
(Photograph, A F Kersting)

108. *The House at Bridlington where Henrietta is reputed to have lodged*, painted in the nineteenth century. (Bridlington Museum)

night. Exhausted by the voyage, she quickly fell into a deep sleep, her faithful companion Mitte the dog lying across the foot of her bed.

At five o'clock in the morning, she was aroused by a noise like thunder. Starting up in alarm, she found Henry Jermyn at her bedside, telling her that four parliamentary ships were bombarding their transport vessels. As she told Charles afterwards, 'One of these ships had done me the favour to flank my house, which fronted the pier, and before I could get out of bed the balls were whistling upon me in such style that you may easily believe I loved not such music. Everybody came to force me to go out, the balls beating so on all the houses that, dressed just as it happened, I went on foot to some distance from the village, to the shelter of a ditch, like those at Newmarket, but before we

109. *The Parliamentary Fleet bombarding Henrietta's troops at Bridlington*, by an unknown artist. (Courtesy of the Director, National Army Museum, London)

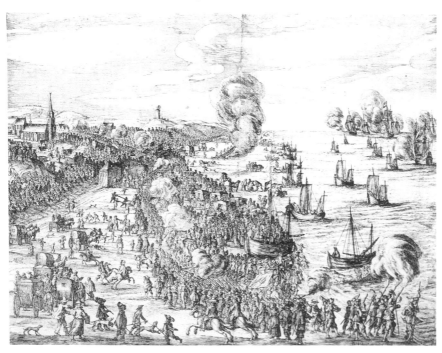

could reach it the balls were singing around us in fine style and a sergeant was killed twenty paces from me'. She did not tell him that, halfway to safety, she horrified her attendants by insisting on running back to the house to rescue Mitte, who had been left behind in all the commotion.

While the soldiers stayed down at the quay, bravely trying to defend their position, she huddled in her ditch, resolving that if the enemy did land, 'I must act the captain, though a little low in stature myself'. Fortunately, that did not prove necessary. Admiral Van Tromp sent the parliamentary vessels a message saying that if they did not stop their bombardment he would fire on them as enemies, even though he was officially neutral. When the Queen asked angrily why he had not acted sooner, he made the excuse that the fog had prevented him from realising what was happening.

As soon as the enemy retired, Henrietta returned to her house on the quay, 'not choosing that they should have the vanity to say that they had made me quit the village'. A larger force of Charles's cavalry arrived later in the day. They escorted her to the town of Bridlington, then went back to unload the ammunition from the ships. While they did so, she sat down and wrote her long letter to her husband describing all that had happened. Her account was 'very exact', she said, 'and after this I am going to eat a little, having taken nothing today but three eggs and slept very little'.

Her greatest wish was to join him at once, but that was not possible because General Fairfax and part of the parliamentary army lay between her and Oxford. She could not even set out for York because she was having difficulty finding waggons to carry her ammunition and her baggage. Hearing that Boynton Hall, three miles from Bridlington, was empty because its owner was away, she moved there and busied herself recruiting men from the surrounding area. As soon as the House of Commons realised that she was back, its members sent a messenger asking why she was raising forces and desiring her to return to London. If she did not, they said, they would do all they could to hinder her proceedings.

110. *Thomas, 3rd Baron Fairfax,* parliamentary commander-in-chief, engraved by W Faithorne after Robert Walker. (National Portrait Gallery, London)

Ignoring this piece of impertinence, she continued to hold conferences with Newcastle and set about raising funds as well as men. She had little enough to offer in return, but she gave lockets, rings and other small trinkets to anyone who lent her money. Noting her absent host's fine plate, she ordered it to be melted down for the royalist cause. When she moved on, she left in exchange a portrait of herself which had been painted in Holland.

Charles was promising to send Prince Rupert to clear a way south for her, so as soon as her waggons were ready she set off for York. She probably lodged in Sir Arthur Ingram's house in the city and there she entertained a series of influential Scotsmen who came to see her. She never had liked the Scots, and their longstanding rivalries made dealing with them all the more difficult. No sooner had the dashing Marquis of Montrose appeared with a scheme for a royalist rising in Scotland than the Marquis of Hamilton arrived to condemn his plan as 'rash, imprudent and unreasonable'. The two men quarrelled violently and even Henrietta could not settle their dispute. She personally favoured Montrose's exciting plan, but in the end she obeyed Charles's instructions and supported Hamilton's campaign for peace.

In March she received distressing news from London. The parliamentarians had burst into her beautiful Somerset House Chapel, seized her priests, smashed her precious furnishings and hurled her statues to the ground. The Chapel had been boarded up and the Capuchins shipped back to France. It was yet another indication of how she would be treated if ever she fell into enemy hands.

When she heard that Charles was negotiating with the rebels again, she was deeply disturbed. In fact, he had no intention of reaching an agreement at that point. He was merely playing for time, but she did not know that, and she wrote to tell him, 'Certainly I wish a peace more than any, and that with greater reason, but I would [desire] the disbanding of the perpetual parliament first'. Indeed, 'if you make a peace and disband your army before there is an end of this perpetual parliament, I am absolutely resolved to go into France, not being willing to fall again into the hands of those people, being well assured that if the power remained with them that it will not be well for me in England'.

Charles took her comments amiss, and wrote her a hurt letter, but she stood her ground. 'If you were as you should be', she replied, 'you would see that all my actions and thoughts have been for you, and that it was only my affection which made me do all that I have done or written . . . and I know well that when I speak to you, you will say I have been more in the right to write as I did than you now think – though I confess I was wrong in something.'

It was all too easy for misunderstandings to arise when he was so far away, with people always at his elbow ready to misinterpret her actions. When Charles wrote again, criticising the way Newcastle was running the campaign in the north, she leaped to the Earl's defence. Everything they both did was for the King, and he would understand that when she explained it in person. Her aim was to bring her own forces to Oxford, so that Charles could march on London with a much augmented army, and while she waited in York she was as busy as ever, toiling from morning till night, deciphering her letters, answering them, attending councils of war, hearing reports from Newcastle and writing constantly to possible friends and allies abroad.

She was sure that Denmark would send aid if only the King would promise them Orkney and Shetland in return and before she had left Holland she had secretly promised the Prince of Orange that she would try to arrange a

marriage between his daughter and Prince Charles. 'I have sent so many dispatches into France and Holland this week', she was telling Charles at the beginning of May, 'that instead of complaining, you should pity me . . . When I see you and can tell you all this, you will say that I am a good little creature and very patient, but I declare to you that being patient is killing me, and were it not for the love of you I would with the greatest truth rather put myself into a convent than live in this manner.'

In spite of her protestations, she was really rather enjoying the excitement of the campaign in Yorkshire and she often boasted about the number of men she was assembling and the success of Newcastle's troops against the rebels. When Pym sent her a message asking her to persuade the King to accept parliament's latest peace offer, she pretended to agree so that she could take advantage of the truce to smuggle a shipment of gunpowder to Oxford.

She was so involved in the struggle that she was not too upset by news of a different kind from France. Her brother Louis XIII died on 14 May. His widow Anne of Austria would now rule on behalf of her small son, Louis XIV. Even the knowledge that the House of Commons had on 23 May voted to impeach her for high treason made relatively little impression on her. She was safe with her own army. Indeed, she had become so involved in the northern campaign that she was reluctant to leave until it was successfully completed. 'Although I am dying to join you', she told Charles, ' . . . I am so enraged to go away without having beaten these scoundrels that if you permit me I will do that and then will go to join you, for if I go away I am afraid that they would not be beaten.'

The King was displeased when he read that. Parliament was threatening to besiege Oxford and Charles needed all available resources for its defence. He told his wife to set out at once, bringing the Earl and his army with her. She was greatly put out. She and Newcastle had already agreed that he would stay

112. Merton College,
Oxford, where
Henrietta stayed:
the College Chapel
from Christchurch
Meadows.
(Photograph,
Priscilla Minay)

in the north to complete his campaign, and so she said that she would go herself with her part of the army.

She set off for Tamworth and Pontefract on 3 June with 3000 footsoldiers, thirty companies of horse, six pieces of cannon and two mortars. Henry Jermyn, now Colonel of her Guards, commanded her forces and she rode at their head, describing herself joyfully to Charles as 'her She-Majesty, General-issima, and extremely diligent, with one hundred and fifty waggons of baggage to govern in case of battle'.

She found the march an exhilarating experience. She was in the saddle all day and she shared meals with her officers in the open country, without any ceremony. She treated them as her brothers and they behaved towards her with affection as well as respect, she said. She began to feel like Alexander the Great. There was danger, of course. She knew that the Earl of Essex would intercept her if he could, but she reached Newark safely and stopped there. Captain Hotham, son of a parliamentary commander who had changed sides, was promising to arrange for Hull and Lincoln to be delivered up to her. The offer was too tempting to ignore and so she waited for almost a month until she heard that the Captain had been captured. With that, she set off south again on 3 July.

Passing through Ashby-de-la-Zouche, Croxall, Walsall and King's Norton, she reached Stratford-on-Avon on the 11th to find Prince Rupert waiting for her. Shakespeare's only surviving daughter entertained her at New Place and she spent the night there, delighted with the thought that she would be with her beloved Charles very soon. They met two days later near Edgehill, after a separation of sixteen months. Prince Charles and Prince James were with the King, and after a blissful reunion they rode off happily to spend the night at Sir Thomas Pope's house at Wroxton.

Plague had broken out in Oxford, so they waited for a day or two at Woodstock until it was judged safe for them to enter the city. They did so to the sound of bells pealing. Crowds lined the streets, trumpets sounded, scholars made long orations and Henrietta received gifts, among them a very welcome purse full of gold. She was to stay in Merton College, where

113. Merton College: the Senior Common Room, which was Henrietta's principal apartment. (Photograph, Royal Commission on the Historical Monuments of England)

apartments had been prepared for her in the Warden's Lodgings. The King took her there himself, escorting her up the fine oak staircase to the handsome room which would be her audience chamber. It overlooked the Great Quadrangle. Her bedchamber was nearby, with steps leading down to the college hall, and her retinue would be accommodated in a series of rooms above the Fellows' Garden. Charles himself occupied Christ Church College not far away.

It was all very overcrowded, but then so was the entire city. As Henrietta rode in she had recognised many familiar faces. The country was at war, but the King was still the centre of his court and he was surrounded by royalist officials, supporters, their wives and their families. They were in very reduced circumstances, of course. As Lady Fanshawe lamented, 'We that till that hour lived in great plenty and great order found ourselves like fishes out of water', and all their talk was of 'losing and gaining towns and men'.

There were soldiers everywhere. Recruits were drilling in the streets and detachments of cavalry clattered through the city on their way to and from their headquarters at Abingdon. The footsoldiers were quartered in the villages in the surrounding countryside and the Oxford colleges were being used not only as lodgings for the noble families but as stores for arms, ammunition, fodder and grain. A mint had been set up at New Inn Hall to melt down plate.

It was a strange world, but Henrietta was so relieved to be back with her husband again that at first she was perfectly content. She and her ladies danced, listened to music and watched theatrical performances put on for them by the students in the college grounds. Charles hunted and played tennis. William Dobson the artist set up a studio in the High Street and painted the portraits of all the fashionable visitors, beginning with the King himself, Prince Charles and Prince Rupert.

Each afternoon Charles came to visit Henrietta, sitting with her in her lodgings or strolling with her in the gardens. They had much to discuss. She

110

told him all about her terrible voyage and the dreary months in Holland, and at her urgent request he gave Henry Jermyn the title Baron Jermyn of St Edmundsbury. She also lost no time in describing the new Dutch plan to help, but Charles was not enthusiastic. Nothing could be done for the present, he said, and she was forced to send that message to The Hague.

She was annoyed, and they disagreed about other issues too. He did not like her friendship with George Digby, whom he did not trust, and he did not seem to appreciate all Newcastle's efforts in the north. More dangerously, he had become too reliant on Prince Rupert, who was as rash as ever, and she thought his recent dealings with the rebels far too lenient. While she was marching south to join him, he had issued a proclamation offering to pardon all those who sought his protection at Oxford. 'You show too much fear', she scolded him, 'and do not do what you had resolved upon.' He should be preparing to march on London, but instead he suddenly decided to go west, hoping to take Gloucester and, with any luck, lure Essex out of the capital.

Henrietta did not like the idea and she blamed Rupert for putting it into Charles's head. He was avoiding the main issue, she complained, and she was nervous of being left behind. It seemed all too likely that parliament would try to besiege Oxford when they heard that the King had left it relatively undefended, and she feared that more than anything. If the city were taken, she would fall into enemy hands and that was to be avoided at all costs. She stormed and raged, but nothing she said had any effect.

Charles undoubtedly relied on Henrietta for moral support, but he did not take her advice on military matters. Ignoring her protests, he set off west and Essex did indeed march to meet him. The two armies confronted each other at Newbury on 20 September 1643. Once again, the battle was indecisive and that same night Charles hurried back to Oxford once more.

Desperate to augment his forces, he now made an alliance with the Irish Roman Catholics. Equally anxious to obtain reinforcements, Parliament signed a treaty with the Scots and on 15 January 1644 the Covenanting army crossed into England. Henrietta at once fired off a series of urgent letters to her friend Newcastle, telling him he must prevent the Scots from 'eating Yorkshire

114. *William, Duke of Newcastle*, commander of Charles I's army in the north, engraved in the eighteenth century by George Vertue after a portrait by Van Dyck.
(Courtauld Institute)

oatcakes': in other words, he must stop them coming any further south. In spite of her bantering tone she was near to despair, for she had just realised that she was pregnant.

Nothing could have been more inconvenient. Essex was threatening to besiege Oxford. She could not possibly stay there, and yet where could she go? The country was in such a state of turmoil that it would be dangerous to travel anywhere. Even as she finished her letter to Newcastle, she heard that Fairfax was marching north to join his army to the Covenanting force. 'Lose no time and do not allow yourself to trifle', she scrawled in a hasty postscript, 'for if the Scots pass the River Tees, I fear that there will be no more remedy. All is lost.'

Suffering from a cold, fever and dreadful pains in her joints, she felt an overwhelming compulsion to flee. Charles tried to dissuade her. She was far too ill to move, he said, but her terror of being taken overcame all other considerations. She did not know where she would find refuge, but go she must. On 17 April the King took her sadly to Abingdon, where they said goodbye. When her coach moved off, she almost fainted, and they had gone several miles before she became aware of her surroundings again. Escorted by Henry Jermyn and a group of armed horsemen, her little cavalcade of coaches and carts moved westwards. If she could get to Bath, perhaps the waters would help.

She was there by 21 April, feeling worse than ever. The jolting of the journey had made the pains in her limbs excruciating and she was unable to find any position in which she could rest. She meant to move to Bristol, but she decided against it and on the 28th she was in Bridgewater, busy with her correspondence once more. An anonymous sympathiser in France was offering to send the King 3000 footsoldiers and 1500 horse. She did not have the strength to write all the details, but she would send Henry Jermyn back to Oxford to explain.

From Bridgewater she went to Exeter, and there she decided to stay. If the worst came to the worst, she would cross to France. Feeling a little safer, she took up her lodgings in the Earl of Bedford's house in the town. Father Philip

115. *Charles I in about 1645*, a miniature by David Des Granges after John Hoskins. (National Portrait Gallery, London)

116. *Bedford House, Exeter*, where Henrietta stayed, drawn by an unknown artist. (The Marquis of Tavistock and The Trustees of the Bedford Estates)

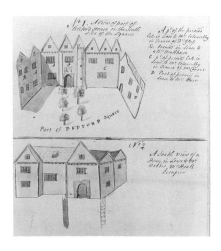

117. Pendennis Castle, a mile south of Falmouth,
where Henrietta spent the night on her way
from Exeter to the coast.
(Photograph, English Heritage)

and Sir Jeffrey Hudson were among those who had accompanied her, and she now sent an urgent letter to her old physician Dr Mayerne, begging him to come to her. He was over seventy, but when the King sent him a note as well, saying simply, 'Mayerne, for the love of me, go to my wife, C.R.' he set out to travel the hundred and seventy miles from London.

The French, meanwhile, had heard what was happening and with character-istic kindness Anne of Austria at once dispatched Madame Peronne the midwife, with a gift of childbed linen and a sum of money. Henrietta kept the linen, but she sent almost all the money to Charles. At the beginning of June, she wrote him a long letter 'which will, I believe, be the last before I am brought to bed (since I am now more than fifteen days in my ninth month) and perhaps it will be the last letter you will ever receive from me'.

Should she die, Lord Jermyn and Father Philip would give him her final message to him. 'If that should happen to me', she said, 'it is a great comfort to me to have written this letter to you. Let it not trouble you, I beg . . . By preparing for the worst, we are never taken by surprise, and good fortune appears so much the greater. Adieu, my dear heart. I hope before I leave to see you once again in the position in which you ought to be. God grant it. I confess that I earnestly desire this, and also that I may be able yet to render you some service.'

She had hardly finished writing when she heard that Essex was marching towards them with the intention of besieging Exeter. This was the very situation she had dreaded, but it was too late for her to travel any further and on 16 June she gave birth to a daughter. The baby was large and healthy, but her own condition was pitiful. 'It seems as though my bowels and stomach weigh more than a hundred pounds and as though I was so tightly squeezed in the region of my heart that I was suffocating', Henrietta told Charles, 'and at times I am like a person poisoned. I can scarcely stir and am doubled up. The same weight is also upon my back, one of my arms has no feeling and my legs and knees are colder than ice. This disease has risen to my head and I cannot see with one eye.'

118. Exeter City Council Act Book recording payment of £200 'to the Queen's Majesty . . . in testimony of the respect unto Her Majesty now in this city', 2 May 1644. (Devon Records Office)

Her illness has been variously diagnosed by twentieth-century historians as rheumatic fever and puerperal sepsis, but the most modern medical opinion suggests a different disease: tuberculosis. The colds, fevers and pains in the joints she suffered while she was in Oxford could be consistent with a sub-acute phase, and the sensations of heaviness and tightness round the heart, the feeling akin to poisoning, the coldness in the limbs and the loss of vision would all fit in. Dr Mayerne was telling people that she could not last much longer, and indeed such an advanced stage of tuberculosis was almost always fatal.

Henrietta, however, was possessed of remarkable determination. She knew that she could not stay where she was. Essex would take the city, Charles would march to her rescue and then they would both be trapped. Anne of Austria might send kind messages, but the French statesmen had no desire for her embarrassing presence and their envoy told her so in no uncertain terms. She therefore thought of returning to Bath in a desperate attempt to recover her health, but Essex refused to grant her a safe-conduct. That left her with no alternative. Welcome or not, she would cross the Channel.

She knew she would be criticised for leaving her husband and her children but, she told Charles in a letter dictated from her bed, 'I shall show you by this last action that nothing is so much in my thoughts as what concerns your preservation, and that my own life is of very little consequence compared with that, for as your affairs stand they would be in danger if you came to help me and I know that your affection would make you risk everything for that'.

On 1 July, she rose from her bed and told her attendants to disguise her in ordinary clothes. Accompanied only by her secretary, her confessor and one of her ladies, she crept out of Exeter. Her baby daugher was left behind in the care of another of Buckingham's nieces, Lady Dalkeith. She could not possibly take the child and her wet-nurse with her on this dangerous expedition. She herself was so weak that they could not travel quickly, and about three miles

out of the city they had to stop, taking refuge in a little hut near the roadside. They crouched there, on a heap of rubbish, with no food, for two days and two nights while soldiers passed to and fro outside. Henrietta even heard one of them promise 50,000 crowns to the man who carried her head to London.

When it seemed safe to continue they made for a cabin in the woods near the Plymouth Road. Lord Jermyn was waiting for them there, with Sir Jeffrey Hudson, some of the Queen's other faithful attendants and her favourite spaniel. They all set off again, two of the men carrying Henrietta in a litter, her secretary walking alongside. A Cornish royalist who saw the sad little procession recognised her and told his wife that it was 'the woefullest spectacle my eyes yet looked on, the most worn and weak, pitiful creature in the world, the poor Queen, shifting for one hour's life longer'. They took her to Pendennis Castle, which was being held for Charles I, and after a day or two there they moved on to Truro. Ten ships were waiting for her in Falmouth Bay, and their French commander was eager to be off, for he had seen three parliamentary vessels close in and he feared that more would appear.

Henrietta dictated a farewell message to the King on 9 July. 'My dear heart', she began, 'this letter is to bid you adieu. If the wind is favourable, I shall set off tomorrow.' She felt so ill that she could not write herself, but she hoped that she would recover her health in France and live to serve him yet. 'I am giving you the strongest proof of love that I can give', she said. 'I am hazarding my life, that I may not incommode your affairs. Adieu, my dear heart. If I die, believe that you will lose a person who has never been other than entirely yours, and who, by her affection, has deserved that you should not forget her.' With that, her usual eloquence failed her, and she ended simply, 'Well, adieu'.

# 9

## THE EXILE

$A$S SOON as Henrietta's ships set sail, the parliamentary vessels bore down upon them and opened fire. She told her captain not to retaliate, for she had no wish to be involved in a naval battle. He must crowd on all his canvas and try to outrun the enemy. If escape seemed impossible, he was to set light to the gunpowder in the hold. She would die in the explosion rather than be taken. As cannon balls crashed around them, her ladies screamed in terror but the Queen remained stoically silent. Somehow, her captain managed to manoeuvre his vessel round so that they could take full benefit of the wind and they went racing across the Channel. As they came within sight of Jersey a shot damaged their rigging. They thought their last hour had come, but a French vessel appeared on the horizon and, mistakenly believing it to be the first of a fleet, the parliamentary ships gave up the chase.

Before the Queen and her companions had time to appreciate their miraculous escape, a storm blew up, tossing their ship about for hours, scattering their escort and finally driving them on to the coast of Brittany, after a voyage of two days. As they rowed in to land in a small boat, the local people came running out of their houses, shouting and brandishing weapons. They thought that the bedraggled sailors were pirates and they were about to drive them back to their ship again when Henrietta called out her true identity and they fell back in horrified disbelief.

Finally convinced that this ill, bent little woman really was Henry IV's daughter come back to them, they helped her over the rocks and led her into one of their thatched cottages. While they did their best to make her comfortable, Henry Jermyn rode for Paris to announce her arrival and beg for doctors to be sent to her at once. Next day all the local nobility came with offers of help and, as soon as she felt able, Henrietta left the coast, travelling slowly through the countryside in a borrowed coach. Crowds lined the roads to stare at her and exclaim over the change in her appearance. Once so pretty, so sparkling and vivacious, she lay weakly back in her seat, unable to stop weeping.

When she was halfway between Nantes and Angers, the doctors arrived, followed swiftly by courtiers from Anne of Austria, bearing messages of welcome and promises of shelter and financial assistance. 'I am so well treated everywhere', said Henrietta, 'that if my lords of London saw it, I think it would make them uneasy.' The physicians advised a visit to the thermal springs at Bourbon l'Archambaut, where she could both bathe and take the waters. The journey there took a month, for every town and village along the way wanted to entertain her with pageants and ceremonies. She was in such pain that she could hardly bear to listen, and when she finally arrived at the spa she collapsed with a high fever. The doctors lanced an abcess in her breast, and it was three weeks before she was able to resume her letters to Charles again, desperate for news of him because she had heard nothing since her departure from England.

She really did think that she was a little better, she wrote. Her limbs were still numb, especially one arm, and for the past three months she had been covered by a rash 'like measles', but her body was less swollen and her head

120. *Bourbon l'Archambaut*, where Henrietta went to recover her health; engraved by Israel. (Bibliothèque Nationale, Paris)

was clearer. 'I do all I can for my life', she said, 'therefore let me have often tidings from you to contribute to it, for believe me they will do so . . . I never expected to see you again, but God is pleased to preserve me still in this world to serve you, as I hope.' Her children were in her thoughts too, and she asked for Prince Charles's measurements so that she could have armour made for him.

Anne of Austria was pressing her to come to Paris, and sent her own favourite lady-in-waiting to serve her. A gentle young widow, Madame de Motteville listened sympathetically as Henrietta recounted her terrible adventures. Her kindness helped and, after some weeks, the doctor said the waters had done all they could for the Queen. They recommended that she drink asses' milk, the classic seventeenth-century treatment for tuberculosis, and they told her that time was what was needed now. She would have to be patient. Perhaps by next spring she would feel herself again.

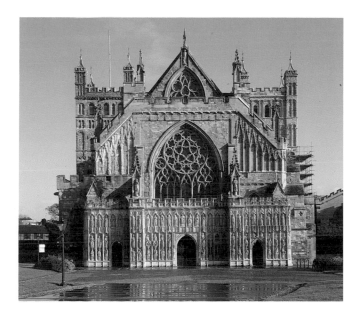

121. Exeter Cathedral, where Princess Henrietta was baptised. (Photograph, A F Kersting)

The combination of the baths and the milk did indeed bring about an improvement in her condition and although she was subject for the rest of her life to fevers and chest infections, it was astonishing that she had recovered at all from such a dangerous illness. Possibly her own strong will to survive was the most significant factor in her return to reasonable health. Her greatest desire, she told people, was to go back to England and as a first step towards that she decided to leave Bourbon and move on to Paris. Perhaps there she would find letters from Charles. She had heard nothing from him since her flight and she was tortured by fears for his safety.

When she arrived in Nevers, they told her that a messenger from England was waiting for her. Pushing aside the supporting arms of her ladies, she hurried to see him, walking unaided for the first time in weeks. Sure enough, the man bore not just one but three letters from the King. The news they contained was mixed. Their affairs in the north had gone badly. Rupert had set off to help the Earl of Newcastle, but they had been defeated at Marston Moor and the Earl, infuriated by Rupert's combination of recklessness and condescension, had thrown up his command and retired to the continent.

Charles himself had fared rather better. Marching west, he had arrived in Exeter to find his wife gone, but Lady Dalkeith, now Countess of Morton, came to him with the baby and his chaplain christened their new princess in Exeter Cathedral, naming her Henrietta. Leaving the infant with her governess, he scattered the enemy before him as he returned to Oxford.

So delighted was Henrietta to hear from him at all that she saw only success in his proceedings and when she wrote back she told him gladly that she would be with him again soon. Kind though they were to her in France, 'I have there [in England] what I have not here, that is YOU, without whom I cannot be happy, and I think I shall never have my health till I see you'. The excitement of questioning his messenger and the exertion of writing back was too much for her. She collapsed again and had to have an abscess in her arm lanced, then just as she was recuperating from that a new crisis arose when Sir Jeffrey Hudson challenged one of her gentlemen, William Crofts, to a duel and shot him dead. She had to intervene hastily to prevent him from being arrested.

When she was able to travel again, her brother Gaston arrived to take her to Paris. Twice married, with a grown-up daughter, he was as volatile as ever but she was fond of him and she was pleased to have his company. Ten miles from

122. *Gaston, Duke d'Orleans*, Henrietta's brother, by Van Dyck.
(In a private collection: photograph, Courtauld Institute)

the capital, they found Anne of Austria waiting, heavier, sadder and dressed in widow's black. Setting aside any lingering memory of their girlhood squabbles, Anne held out her arms with loving sympathy and they embraced each other fondly. From then onwards, Anne was an unfailing source of comfort and support to Henrietta.

The Queen Regent proudly presented her two small sons, Louis XIV and his little brother Philip, Duke d'Orleans. There were welcoming speeches, and then they rode into Paris together. Anne installed Henrietta in comfortable apartments in the Louvre, made over St Germain to her and organised a great service of thanksgiving in Notre Dame for her safe return. She arranged a pension for her, invited her to balls and receptions and, in short, did everything she could to alleviate the pain of exile.

The day after the thanksgiving, she introduced Henrietta to her chief adviser and intimate friend, Cardinal Jules Mazarin. This urbane, middle-aged Italian had been carefully groomed for his position as chief minister by his predecessor Cardinal Richelieu, and all real power lay with him. Delighted with his affability, Henrietta immediately began to ply him with requests for military aid for her husband. She soon realised, however, that although he was willing to promise everything, he would do nothing. He had no more desire than Richelieu to see a powerful, united Britain. Her task was not going to be easy, but she was resolved to persevere.

She regarded her stay in France as an interlude, a period to recover and gain assistance rather than a permanent return home. She might chat pleasantly to the courtiers and do a little entertaining, but her mind was fixed on England. She lived for her husband's letters and she was devoted to his cause. Somehow, she would gather the men and money he needed, and then she would return and rescue him from his enemies. Apart from her emotional involvement with him, her pride would not allow her to accept the role of the humble exile. She was Queen of England. When she said 'we' she meant herself, her husband and her children, and when she spoke of 'my country' she was referring to Britain.

She was surrounded by large numbers of British in her household. Lord Jermyn was always by her side, ready to make himself useful, with Abraham Cowley, the poet, acting as his personal secretary. The Duchess of Richmond and the Countess of Denbigh led her ladies still, and Father Philip the confessor had come with her to France. Apart from these permanent companions, impoverished royalist exiles like Newcastle began to arrive from all over the continent, hoping for financial assistance. Soon, her pension was dwindling away in gifts to them and, more importantly, in purchasing the supplies Charles so desperately needed.

Unfortunately, the French were not the only people who were unwilling to help. The Prince of Orange no longer saw any benefit in an alliance with England, the Irish situation was complicated by strife between the Roman Catholics and Protestants, and when she applied directly to Rome, her envoy, the flamboyant Sir Kenelm Digby, made such a bad impression that the Pope decided he must be deranged and refused to have anything to do with him.

Overworked and frustrated, Henrietta fell seriously ill that spring with a high fever and a flux. For a time her life seemed in danger, but by the beginning of May she was able to tell Charles, 'God has still pleased to leave me in this world to do you service . . . I . . . rather wish that I may see you again before I die . . . for all that troubled me during my illness was that I was dying far from you, otherwise I did not care about it much'.

123. *Cardinal Mazarin*, Anne of Austria's chief adviser, by Mignard. (Musée Condé, Chantilly: photograph, Lauros-Giraudon)

124. *Abraham Cowley*, the poet, secretary in Henrietta's household, by Sir Peter Lely. (National Portrait Gallery, London)

Even before her convalescence was over, she was hard at work again, trying in vain to hire French mercenaries and negotiating fruitlessly with Denmark, Norway and Sweden. That summer brought disaster to the King's cause when he and Prince Rupert encountered Oliver Cromwell and his New Model Army at Naseby. Pym was dead now, and parliament began to look to this forty-three-year-old East Anglian squire for leadership. When the battle was over, a thousand royalists lay dead on the field and another five thousand were wounded or captured. Further reverses followed when Prince Rupert angered the King by surrendering Bristol to the enemy, and Montrose was defeated at Philiphaugh on the very day that Henrietta had arranged for a *Te Deum* to be sung in Paris in honour of his victories.

The only hope now seemed to be for Charles to turn to the Scots once more. For religious and nationalistic reasons they were tiring of their alliance with the English parliament. Perhaps their old allegiance to the monarchy would outweigh their distaste for royal policies of the more recent past. Mazarin took this view too and, having no desire to see parliament win an outright victory, he sent an emissary over to negotiate an agreement between the King and the Scots. After prolonged discussions, Charles slipped out of Oxford in disguise and went to the Scottish camp at Newark.

On the eve of his departure he wrote urging Henrietta to 'continue the same active endeavours for Prince Charles as thou hast done for me, and whine not for my misfortune in a retired way, but, like thy father's daughter, vigorously assist Prince Charles to regain his own'. At the same time, he ordered the Prince to join his mother in France, where he was to be ruled by her in everything but religion. Prince James, left behind in Oxford, was taken prisoner when parliament captured the city and sent to join Henry and Elizabeth.

Charles regretted his decision almost at once. Instead of receiving him honourably and restoring him, the Scots demanded that he take the National Convenant and impose Presbyterianism on England. He refused, and as a result he found himself treated as a prisoner and harangued every day by Scottish divines determined to make him change his mind. Henrietta was

120

125. *Oliver Cromwell*, Lord
Protector of England,
painted by Robert Walker,
about 1649.
(National Portrait
Gallery, London)

126. *Charles Prince of Wales*,
in 1648, by Des Granges.
(The Duke of Buccleuch and
Queensberry KT:
photograph, *Scotland's Story*)

desperately afraid that he was about to throw away their last chance. Surely he, who had already compromised so many of his principles, could compromise once again to save his life and allow them to be together?

He did not see it in that light. By his coronation oath he had sworn to defend the Church of England with its bishops. It was all part of his theory of Divine Right. Without them the Church would crumble and the monarchy would be more readily overthrown. He would do almost anything for her. 'Dear heart . . .', he told her, 'there is no danger which I will not hazard or pains that I will not undergo to enjoy the happiness of thy company', but he would not agree to Presbyterianism being introduced into England.

For over a year their letters went back and forth arguing the point, until in the end Charles forbade her to discuss the matter any further. 'The Queen will break my heart if she any more undertake to obtain my consent for Presbyterian government', he told her, 'for if she once should openly condemn me of wilfulness, but in one point, I should not be able to support my daily miseries.' Differ as they might, she remained his sole source of comfort and support. 'Above all', he told her on another occasion, 'thou must make my acknowledgments to the Queen of England (for none else can do it), it being her love that maintains my life, her kindness that upholds my courage, which makes me eternally hers.'

If Charles's obstinacy was a continual torment, her favourite son was proving almost equally difficult. Instead of joining her as instructed, the

121

Prince of Wales had sought refuge in Jersey and was refusing to leave. His council of advisers had no doubt put him up to this, Henrietta decided, for they feared her influence over him. However, she would not allow them to dictate to her. She complained to the King, sent Lord Jermyn to fetch the recalcitrant Prince and at last was able to welcome him to Paris.

He was a tall, well-made, black-haired, fifteen-year-old now. Henrietta was overjoyed to see him again, and she immediately took him to court to show him off to Anne of Austria and all the other notabilities. Handsome though he undoubtedly was, he was hardly a social success. It was bad enough that he seemed very taciturn by nature, but even worse was the fact that he did not speak or even seem to understand French. His mother had hopes of marrying him to her niece, a wealthy heiress, but Gaston's daughter was distinctly unimpressed and nothing came of the scheme.

Although Henrietta was disappointed, soon afterwards she received the most delightful surprise. Since her departure, the Countess of Morton had been caring devotedly for Princess Henrietta. That summer, parliament ordered her to hand the child over so that she could be kept in captivity with

127. *Henrietta* [on right] *and Anne of Austria*, by P. Mignard. This picture was painted for the Church of Notre Dame de Bonne Nouvelle in Paris, which Anne had founded, and which was demolished in 1823.
(Photograph, Bulloz)

James, Henry and Elizabeth. Lady Morton could not bear to do that. Dressing herself in a tattered gown, she stuffed the back with pieces of linen to conceal her tall, elegant figure and then, posing as her French valet's wife, she set off with him to walk to Dover. They took it in turn to carry the two-year-old Princess. She was disguised in a boy's old clothes and they addressed her as 'Pierre'. 'Not Pierre! Princess!' the child exclaimed angrily, plucking at her dirty garments with a fierce frown. When at last they arrived at Dover, the authorities paid little attention to the family of French beggars, as they thought, and they were able to board a ship unchallenged.

As soon as they landed in France they send word to the Queen. Henrietta could hardly believe it. She had not seen her baby since she was a fortnight old. Delightedly she sent coaches and servants to fetch the travellers, and when they were reunited she gazed with wonder at the beautiful, dark-haired, intelligent child who so much resembled herself as she once had been. As a compliment to the Queen Regent, she announced that her daughter would be known as Henrietta Anne. The Prince of Wales, greatly taken with her, called her Minette, which means Little Puss.

It was as well that there was some cheerful aspect to her life, for her husband was being more exasperating than ever. He had been negotiating with the rebels again and he had even offered to hand over control of the militia for twenty years. When she heard that, Henrietta was furious. Terrified that he would give away more and more without realising the consequences, she said repeatedly that she would enter a convent rather than go back under such circumstances, and her reproaches held a new bitterness. 'You stick at [abolishing] bishops and episcopacy', she raged, 'yet you go ahead and betray your posterity. I tell you for the last time, if you concede anything more, you are lost, and I will never again return to England.'

His response was to speak of escaping to France. She was appalled at the thought of him abandoning their cause and she told him plainly that he must not think of it unless all else failed. In any event, the French did not want him. His presence would be far too embarrassing. Finally, his terms were rejected and the Covenanters, after receiving £100,000 from their English allies, handed him over to parliament and departed for home. By now, parliament and the English army were at odds with one another, and a few weeks later the army seized the King and took him to London.

Henrietta hardly knew where to turn. Mazarin had finally abandoned any pretence of assisting, the Pope had written Charles off, and the Dutch were not in the least interested. She sent one of her chaplains to Ireland to see if something could be done there, but her efforts ended in failure. She then sent Lord Jermyn's kinsman Sir John Berkeley to try to mediate between the King and the army, but Charles seemed to feel that it was beneath his dignity to negotiate with mere army officers.

He remained convinced that he could not lose the struggle because God was on his side. After much tortured thought, he had worked out what had happened. Angry at Strafford's death all these years before, God had decided to punish both King and people by allowing civil war to descend on them. In the end, of course, the monarchy would be restored. Meanwhile, he played for time, doing his best to exploit the differences between Scots and English, parliament and army. Soon, no one trusted him.

In the winter of 1647 he managed to escape and made for Carisbrooke Castle on the Isle of Wight, believing its captain to be loyal to him. He was not, and Charles found himself a prisoner once more. By this time, many royalist Scots

128. *Minette as a child*, by C Mellan.
(The National Swedish Art Museums, Stockholm)

were horrified at the turn events had taken, and the Duke of Hamilton offered to lead an expedition from Scotland to rescue him. When Henrietta heard that, she immediately redoubled her fundraising efforts.

She had already been sending most of her money to Charles. Now she dismissed servants, sold furnishings, did away with her fine coaches and horses and pawned the last of her jewels in Holland. The Venetian ambassador saw her one day waiting in Mazarin's outer office with tears in her eyes. She was still trying to enlist his assistance. Her confessor, old Father Philip, died that autumn and to add to her troubles civil war, the Fronde, broke out in France as a result of discontent with the Cardinal's rule.

She was desperately anxious because the Prince of Wales was about to join the Scottish royalist campaign. When he went, she retired to her favourite Carmelite convent in the Faubourg St Jacques to pray for him, and there she was visited by Madame de Motteville and one of her friends. They were grieved to see her sad condition. She was sitting in a little chamber, busily writing dispatches, and she spoke to them about her terrible anxieties. She also showed them her little gold drinking-cup. It was the only valuable she had left.

She did have one piece of good news soon after. With the aid of a faithful servant, her son James disguised himself as a girl, boarded a ship and escaped to Holland where he joined his sister Mary. He would come to France soon. She was just making plans to send him to Ireland when word came that the Scottish royalist army had been destroyed at Preston. Charles at last accepted the fact that he might not live to rule again and Henrietta received a letter from him telling her he would not be much longer in this world. She should cease her efforts to save him, for they would be to no purpose.

She read his words with such a sense of shock that she almost collapsed, and her alarmed attendants thought that she was dying. When she recovered, she wrote back saying that she shared his sorrows. If he were to die, she had no wish to live without him, but she could not accept that his cause was lost. She would go on doing her utmost to help him in every possible way.

There was little she could do, for the Fronde was raging around the capital and Anne of Austria and the court withdrew to St Germain. Henrietta, of no political importance in the struggle, would be safe enough in the Louvre, it was thought, so there she stayed. She kept up a brave front, but her ladies reported that 'her nights are more sad than usual'. She was so poor that when Cardinal de Retz visited her in January he found her sitting in four-year-old Minette's chilly bedchamber. 'You find me keeping my Henrietta company', she said, 'I would not let the poor child rise today as we have no fire.' The Cardinal was horrified, and he at once arranged for her to have some money.

When the rebels seized Paris, Anne of Austria's army blockaded the city and Henrietta was afraid that she was going to be cut off from all news of England. She wrote urgently to Lord Fairfax, asking for a safe-conduct so that she could join Charles, and she wrote in similar terms to the speakers of both houses of parliament. 'I dare not promise myself that they will accord me the liberty of going', she told Monsieur de Grignan, who was to carry these message. 'I wish it too much to assure myself of it, at a time when so little of what I desire succeeds', but she felt she had to try. She was unaware that, three days earlier, the House of Commons had passed an act setting up a court to try the King on a charge of treason. When her letters arrived in London, the Commons put them aside unopened and they were found among the official records thirty-five years later, still sealed.

Desperate for news, she decided to go to St Germain, for the French court was still in touch with the outside world. Taking Minette, she crept out of the Louvre, but as they made their way through the gardens of the Tuileries they were stopped and forced to turn back. While she waited in an agony of suspense, Charles was tried in Westminster Hall, and on 27 January he was sentenced to death.

The following day he was taken to St James's Palace and Princess Elizabeth and Prince Henry were brought to him. They both burst into tears when they saw him. Urging them not to grieve, he told his daughter to assure Henrietta that his thoughts had never strayed from her and that his love would remain unaltered until the end. Taking Henry on his knee, he warned him never to accept the throne as long as Prince Charles was still alive. 'I will sooner be torn in pieces first!' Henry cried.

The King then wrote a long last letter to his eldest son, telling him to respect, love and protect 'your mother, who hath many ways deserved well of me and chiefly in this, that having been a means to bless me with so many hopeful children (all which, with their mother, I recommend to your love and care) she

129. *Charles I at his Trial*, by Edward Bower, 1648.
(Reproduced by gracious permission of Her Majesty The Queen)

hath been content with incomparable magnanimity and patience to suffer both for and with me and you'.

On 30 January 1649, he walked for the last time through St James's Park, and into his Banqueting House at Whitehall. He had put on two shirts that morning, so that people would not see him shiver from the cold and think that he was afraid. He was, indeed, entirely calm. He prayed and took a little refreshment and then at two o'clock in the afternoon he stepped out of a window in the Banqueting House and on to the black-draped scaffold which had been erected outside. There, he made his final speech. Since the beginning of his trial, his stutter had completely disappeared and he spoke without hesitation. The fact that he was submitting to punishment was not a sign of guilt, he insisted. Parliament had started the war, not he, and thinking of Strafford he went on, 'I will only say this. That an unjust sentence that I suffered to take effect is punished now by an unjust sentence on me . . . '

He took off his Order of the Garter, put a white satin cap on his head to keep back his hair and placed his neck on the block. 'I go from a corruptible to an incorruptible crown, where no disturbances can be; no disturbances in the world', he said. The masked executioner stepped forward and Charles died under one swift stroke of the axe. When his head was held up for all to see, a

130. The Banqueting House, Whitehall, where Charles was executed.
(Photograph, PSA Photographic Unit)

groan rose from the huge crowd and men and women rushed forward to dip their handkerchiefs in his blood. The King was buried in St George's Chapel, Windsor, ten days later.

They did not know how to break the news to Henrietta. Lord Jermyn tried. He told her about the proceedings in Westminster Hall and the sentence of death, but when he saw her expression his courage failed him, and he said that the crowds at Whitehall had risen up at the last moment and saved the King. She wept with relief. The truth could not be kept from her forever, of course, and a day or two later, when Father de Gamache the Capuchin was told to stay with her after he had pronounced grace at the dinner table, he felt a dreadful sense of foreboding. Throughout the meal the Queen's companions kept up a general conversation, but she could hardly listen to them. She had sent yet another gentleman to St Germain to see if there was any news, and she could not understand why he had not returned. At last, Lord Jermyn remarked sadly that if the news had been good, the man would have been back by now.

'What is it, then?' the Queen asked sharply, staring at him. 'I perceive plainly that you know!' Hanging his head, he mumbled that he did know something. She urged him to go on. He must tell her. He could hardly find the words but at last, after a lengthy preamble, he blurted out the truth. The King was dead. Henrietta stood as though transfixed. Everyone else was in tears, but she remained motionless, unable to utter a word, 'like a statue', said Father de Gamache. He, Lord Jermyn and all her other devoted servants gathered round and spoke to her, trying to rouse her, but she seemed unaware that they were there. Finally, they all fell silent, grouped around her in attitudes of sympathy and grief.

131. *The Execution of Charles I,* by an unknown artist. The Banqueting House can be seen in the background. (On loan to the Scottish National Portrait Gallery from the Earl of Rosebery)

When several hours had passed, they were seriously alarmed about her, for she was still in a state of profound shock. Someone had the idea of sending for her old friend the Duchess de Vendôme, wife of her half-brother, César. They had been close friends since childhood. The Duchess came, in tears. She took Henrietta's hand, kissed it affectionately and spoke quietly to her. At last, the Queen began to weep.

132. *Henry Jermyn*, Henrietta's faithful adviser, painted by an artist of the studio of Lely.
(Cirencester Park: photograph, Courtauld Institute)

133. *Françoise, Duchess of Vendôme*, wife of Henrietta's half-brother and her own close friend, from the Book of Hours of Catherine de Medici (which has seventeenth-century portraits added to it).
(Bibliothèque Nationale, Paris, Department of Manuscripts, nouvelles acquisitions latines 82)

# 10

## QUEEN MOTHER

*H*ENRIETTA THOUGHT that she would die too. She lay in bed for several days, torturing herself with regret that she had not been with Charles, and then she sought refuge in the Carmelite convent, where she prayed over and over again, 'Lord, thou hast permitted it, therefore will I submit myself with all my strength'. After several weeks, Father de Gamache came to beg her to return to the world. Her family needed her, he said, and that was an appeal which she could not resist. She went back to the Louvre.

She was never the same again, of course, for, as she told all her visitors, she had lost not only her husband and her King but her friend. The intimate, loving, trusting partnership which had so sustained her was gone and could never be replaced. She would find other causes to fight for and other people to order about, but she was irrevocably changed. As long as Charles was alive, she was still, in part at least, the flirtatious, outrageous little girl he loved. Now, that aspect of her nature was gone.

She did not lose her sense of humour, it was true. Madame de Motteville noticed that even as Henrietta was busy recounting a dreadful adventure from her past, with tears in her eyes, she would suddenly burst out laughing when some absurd detail came to mind. Despite her merriment and her entertaining stories, however, her friends found a new depth to her character. She had always been kind and helpful, but there was in her now an even greater sympathy and a sensitive understanding. They went to her for support and advice, and if her situation at court as a financially dependent exile was hard to endure, she bore it with grace and an exquisite tact.

The only people who did not appreciate her, it sometimes seemed, were her own sons and daughters, but then it is a rare mother who has no stormy scenes with her adolescent children. Moreover, Henrietta's family relationships were complicated by her unique circumstances. She had not raised her offspring personally and their childhood had been brutally ended by the Civil War. Both Charles and James left the schoolroom to see active service and by the time they arrived in Paris they were used to the comradeship of army officers and

134. *Henry, Duke of Gloucester,* Henrietta's son, after a portrait of about 1659 by
Johann Boeckhorst.
(National Portrait Gallery, London)

the deference of their advisers. When Henrietta ordered them about and expected them to listen meekly to her, they rebelled.

Charles was reasonably amenable at first, in part because he was sorry for her and also because he and she were united in their desire to see him take his proper place in the world. He was King Charles II now, and his great objective was to drive out the usurper Oliver Cromwell and regain his rightful throne. Money and allies would be needed. Well-versed in the frustrating business of trying to enlist support, Henrietta set about writing her letters again.

By the spring of 1650, everything was ready. Charles would go to Scotland to lead a royalist rising. He set sail in May only to be defeated by Cromwell at Dunbar, but he did not give up. He endured the company of the censorious Presbyterians for another year and then they marched into England together. Cromwell crushed their army once more at Worcester on 3 September 1651. After the battle Charles vanished. For six long weeks no one knew what had become of him and Henrietta was convinced that she had lost him too, when he suddenly reappeared in France, unharmed but greatly altered.

Her thin, dark boy had become an impressive man, six feet three inches tall, muscular and commanding. Beneath his lighthearted manner his friends sensed a deep melancholy and an impenetrable reserve. He no longer consulted his mother about his business. He listened courteously to her advice, but he made it clear that he did not want her meddling in his affairs. When she tried to tell him what to do, he simply walked out of the room. Finally he went off to Holland to stay with his sister Mary.

Henrietta still had James, of course, but he was not the most harmonious companion. He argued with her constantly, and when he did not get his own way, he sulked for days. After one particularly bitter quarrel, he ran away to Flanders to join the army, and although they eventually made up their differences, it was clear that he was determined to do as he pleased himself.

Her third son, Henry, was still a prisoner in England, but late in 1652 parliament finally released him and he arrived in Paris early the following year, to his mother's great joy. She had not seen him since he was just over a year old: now he was twelve. She was delighted with 'this little cavalier', she told her sister Christine, and the whole French court came to admire him. He settled down happily at first, but when he had been with her for about a year, she could no longer resist the temptation of trying to convert him to Roman Catholicism. She had promised Charles II that she would not interfere with his religion, but since her husband's death she had become increasingly anxious to save the souls of those she loved, and Anne of Austria was continually asking her, 'Has he turned yet?'

A fearful quarrel ensued, for Henry was a staunch Protestant. When she arranged to send him away to a Roman Catholic school, he appealed to Charles, who was furious. Rebuking his mother, he sent his friend the Duke of Ormonde to fetch Henry to Holland. The boy gladly made his preparations to leave, and went to say goodbye to Henrietta. He met her outside the palace, on her way to Mass. She had been deeply wounded by what she saw as his defiance and when he knelt before her to ask her blessing, she turned her head away, exclaiming, 'Never let me see your face again!' After attending a Protestant service, he went back to the palace to find his horses had been led out of the stables, his bed had been stripped and the cooks had been told not to prepare any dinner for him. He went to the Duke of Ormonde, and they left at once.

135. *Princess Mary*, Henrietta's daughter, by Hannemann, 1660. (Reproduced by gracious permission of Her Majesty The Queen)

Not long afterwards, to Henrietta's deep distress, Mazarin signed a peace treaty with Cromwell. One result of the agreement was that her sons would not be able to return to her in France, nor could they fight in the French armies, for they could not be seen to support a country which recognised the parliamentary regime in Britain. Charles, James and Henry therefore enlisted in the Spanish armies in Flanders against the French. Henrietta heard little from them.

Her three daughters could have been a comfort, but the two elder girls were far away. Mary had grown up into an elegant young lady of fashion, living happily with her husband, Prince William, in The Hague and regretting only that she had so far been unable to bear him a child. After at least one serious miscarriage, she found herself pregnant again in 1651 and it seemed that, this time, she would carry the baby to full term. Just as she was approaching her time, William caught smallpox and died. His delicate, posthumous son was born eight days later and named after him.

Henrietta was distressed for Mary and also for herself. 'It seems that God wishes to show me that I should detach myself altogether from this world, by taking from me those who would lead me to think of it', she said, and she added, 'The loss of my son-on-law makes me see this, for in him were placed all my hopes for my son's restoration'. Mary did pay her a visit eventually, revelling in all the entertainments of the French court and regretting the necessity of returning to unsophisticated Holland, but mother and daughter were never close, although Mary was adored by all her brothers.

Princess Elizabeth did not manage to join her family abroad. A gentle, sensitive girl, she never really recovered from her father's death, and when her captors moved her to Carisbrooke Castle, the scene of his long imprisonment, the shock was too great. She died soon afterwards. Like her sister Anne, she had been suffering from tuberculosis, but Henrietta had no doubts that the real cause of her death was a broken heart.

Anxiety and sorrow made her ill that winter, but at least she had Minette for consolation, and no bitterness ever marred that relationship. From the day that the child was brought to her in France they were hardly ever apart, and Father de Gamache in fact commented that Henrietta 'loved her daughter with an excessive fondness'. He was entrusted with the little girl's religious instruction, for Charles I had long ago agreed that she could be brought up as a Roman Catholic. This was important, not only for spiritual reasons. Her future obviously lay in France, and Henrietta dreamed of making a brilliant marriage for her.

To that end, she spared no trouble or expense in ensuring that she was suitably educated: she even borrowed her sister's musician, Monsieur Flaill, to teach Minette to play the harp. The child's quickness, her rapid progress and her endearing ways were Henrietta's principal pleasure during these long years when the prospect of her son's restoration to the throne seemed to be growing ever more remote.

She and Minette had several changes of residence at that time. At first, they stayed in the Louvre or at St Germain, but Anne of Austria decided that there was no longer any room for them in her son's principal palace and she gave them Cardinal Richelieu's old house instead. The Palais Royal was handsome and comfortable but Henrietta missed life in the country and when St Germain was no longer available to her she decided to buy her own country mansion. She found a charming little castle at Colombe, just seven miles north of Paris, and she and her daughter settled down happily there.

She also had apartments in a religious foundation. Anxious to divert her mind from her grief after Charles's death, she decided to found a convent. Madame de Motteville's sister and several other friends belonged to the Order of the Visitation. Established some forty years before for daughters of the aristocracy, it allowed its nuns to live under a rule less stringent than that of the Carmelites, for instance. There was already a house in Paris, but there was no reason why she could not open another outside the city.

As she drove about the countryside looking for suitable premises, she came upon the beautiful mansion at Chaillot which had belonged to her old acquaintance Marshal de Bassompierre. He was dead now and the property was for sale. For some years past it had been rented out by his creditors as a highly dubious place of entertainment, so Henrietta was able to secure it at a considerably reduced price. She had very little money, but with Anne of Austria's help she persuaded friends to contribute. She then set about the delightful task of redecorating Chaillot, hurrying out two and three times a week with fine furnishings from Paris.

Her bedchamber at the front of the house was done up in fawn and black, with an oval painting of the Virgin, Christ and John the Baptist on the wall, and her little cabinet next door had a rather grand crimson and gold couch. From the best of intentions, she made the nuns' chambers so comfortable that, when they saw them, they declared that they could not possibly live in such luxury. In fact, they marched up to the attics, and refused to come down again until the sumptuous furnishings had been taken away. A week later, the first

136. *The Convent of St Mary, at Chaillot,* founded by Henrietta. This engraving is after Lantara. (Bibliothèque Nationale, Paris)

High Mass was held in the convent chapel, in the presence of Anne of Austria. Thereafter, Henrietta and Minette spent weeks at a time at Chaillot.

In 1658 Oliver Cromwell died and Henrietta was surprised to find that she felt little elation. Perhaps it was because 'my heart is so wrapped up in melancholy as to be incapable of receiving any [joy]', she remarked, 'or that I do not as yet perceive any good advantages likely to accrue to us from it'.

137. *Charles II dancing at The Hague, on the eve of the Restoration,* with his sister Mary, painted by H Janssens. (Reproduced by gracious permission of Her Majesty The Queen)

138, *General George Monck*, who arranged Charles II's restoration, engraved by David Loggan in 1661.
(National Portrait Gallery, London)

Nevertheless, when Richard Cromwell succeeded as Lord Protector, it soon became evident that he was a very different man from his father and Charles II's prospects improved dramatically. Her spirits rising, Henrietta offered to help. Fearing she might do something rash, he wrote back counselling caution, but by the winter of 1659 his affairs were going so well that he felt it safe to visit her at Colombe.

He had not seen his family for six years, and he caused great hilarity by embracing one of his mother's ladies by mistake for Minette. He was in high good humour, and the reunion went well. Henrietta asked him to give Lord Jermyn a peerage, and he made him Earl of St Albans. Mother and son spent several days talking together, and by the time he left, they were on the best of terms. Meanwhile, Richard Cromwell had proved increasingly incompetent and many Britons were convinced that the monarchy must be restored. As Charles rode away from Colombe, General George Monck was already marching to London with an army, to prepare the way for his return.

Charles entered London in triumph on 29 May 1660, his thirtieth birthday, accompanied by James and Henry. Henrietta ordered bonfires to be lit in her gardens at Colombe and next day she held a fireworks party at the Palais Royal after attending Mass at Chaillot. Suddenly she was transformed from an impoverished exile into the mother of a ruling monarch. Everyone wanted to congratulate her, and royalists were arriving from all over the continent, asking for letters of recommendation to Charles. She and Minette were caught up in a delightful whirl of excitement.

Charles was anxious for them to join him in England. Mary was coming over from Holland and when they too arrived his family would at last be together again. Henrietta was reluctant. When her husband was alive, her greatest desire had been to return, but since the terrible events of 1649 she could not think of England without pain and although she did not say so openly, she shrank from the thought of going to London. There was another reason, too. Fifteen-year-old Minette had reached a crucial point in her life.

Ideally, Henrietta would have like her to marry Louis XIV, but she had been forced to accept that this was not possible. Anne of Austria had selected her own niece, the Spanish Infanta, for his wife. Anne did have a younger son, however, and she had indicated that when the court returned from Spain with Marie Thérèse, Philip, Duke d'Orleans might well ask for Minette's hand. This

139. *Charles II enters London*, by Dirk Stoop.
(Museum of London)

was no time for the Princess to leave. They therefore stayed on in France and, sure enough, the day before the Infanta's state entry into Paris, Anne of Austria came in person to say that Philip wanted to marry Minette.

Henrietta wept tears of joy, although Philip was not exactly the ideal bridegroom. A strange, dark, intense, young man, he had hitherto shown no interest in the opposite sex. As a child he had liked nothing better than dressing in girls' clothing and now, at nineteen, he spent all his time with his male favourites. Henrietta had known her nephew from his early childhood, however, and he and she were fond of each other. Moreover, when the marriage was announced, he astonished everyone by behaving as though he were passionately in love with Minette.

He was reluctant to part with her, even for a few weeks, but Charles II was insisting that she and her mother should postpone their visit to London no longer. Even then, Henrietta seemed reluctant, and there was a new delay when tragic news arrived from England. Prince Henry had died of smallpox. He and his mother had been corresponding, somewhat frostily, since their quarrel, but now there could be no personal reconciliation. The Queen was deeply distressed and she might have been tempted to remain in France that winter but for a new domestic crisis.

140. *Philip, Duke d'Orleans*, nephew of Henrietta and husband of Minette, attributed to Mignard.
(In a private collection: photograph, Giraudon)

135

# HENRIETTA'S DESCENDANTS

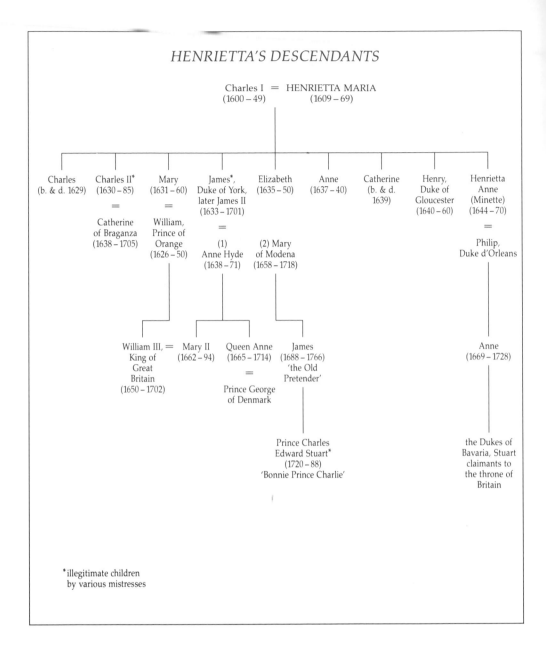

Charles I = HENRIETTA MARIA
(1600 – 49)        (1609 – 69)

Charles
(b. & d. 1629)

Charles II*
(1630 – 85)
=
Catherine
of Braganza
(1638 – 1705)

Mary
(1631 – 60)
=
William,
Prince of
Orange
(1626 – 50)

James*,
Duke of York,
later James II
(1633 – 1701)
=
(1)
Anne Hyde
(1638 – 71)

Elizabeth
(1635 – 50)

(2) Mary
of Modena
(1658 – 1718)

Anne
(1637 – 40)

Catherine
(b. & d.
1639)

Henry,
Duke of
Gloucester
(1640 – 60)

Henrietta
Anne
(Minette)
(1644 – 70)
=
Philip,
Duke d'Orleans

William III, = Mary II
King of      (1662 – 94)
Great
Britain
(1650 – 1702)

Queen Anne
(1665 – 1714)
=
Prince George
of Denmark

James
(1688 – 1766)
'the Old
Pretender'

Anne
(1669 – 1728)

Prince Charles
Edward Stuart*
(1720 – 88)
'Bonnie Prince Charlie'

the Dukes of
Bavaria, Stuart
claimants to
the throne of
Britain

*illegitimate children
by various mistresses

It was bad enough that Charles was apparently flaunting his latest mistress, Lady Castlemaine, instead of seeking a respectable bride, but James's behaviour was even worse. He had gone to the King in tears one day to confess that he had secretly married his mistress Anne Hyde, because she was eight months pregnant. Henrietta was appalled at his stupidity. He could have kept the girl as a mistress: there had been no need to make her his wife. It did not help when people pointed out that Anne was the daughter of Charles's chief adviser, Edward Hyde. Henrietta had always loathed the man, whom she suspected of turning her son against her, and he was far too low-born to be the father-in-law of the Duke of York. Announcing grimly, 'I go tomorrow for England to marry my son the King and try to unmarry the other', she set out for the coast.

141. *James II and his wife, Anne Hyde,* by Sir Peter Lely.
(National Portrait Gallery, London)

Accompanied by Henry Jermyn and her retinue, she and Minette embarked at Calais, promising Philip that they would be back by Christmas. The weather was so calm that the crossing took two days. James, now Lord High Admiral of England, sailed out to meet her with the entire fleet, and Charles welcomed her off Dover, accompanied by Mary and Prince Rupert. In a poignant repetition of her previous journey thirty-five years before, Henrietta spent her first night back in Dover Castle, before travelling to London.

It had been arranged that she would enter the city quietly, because the sight of Charles I's Roman Catholic Queen returning might cause disturbances, but by the time she reached Lambeth the Thames was thronged with craft of every

142. *Princess Henrietta Anne* (Minette), painted by Samuel Cooper, the miniaturist, during her visit to London.
(By courtesy of the Board of Trustees of the Victoria and Albert Museum)

kind and the banks were crowded with people. She crossed the river and landed at the Privy Stairs at Whitehall. She could not bear to look towards the Banqueting House, and when she was led into her old apartments she cried out in anguish, 'Ruin and desolation are around and about me!' However, Minette's presence helped, and two hours later she was taking the Princess on a tour of the palace.

In the weeks that followed, the royal family went to concerts, banquets, plays and celebrations. They dined in public together, played cards in their own apartments and met a host of old friends. Henrietta's audience-chamber was crowded with people each day and almost everyone was delighted with her charm, her sincerity, her ability to remember names and her kind enquiries after friends and relatives. One of the few visitors to remain unimpressed was Samuel Pepys. He watched her dine and thought her 'a very little, plain old woman and nothing more in her presence in any respect nor garb than any ordinary woman'.

One of the first places she visited was her old home, Somerset House, sadly dilapidated now. 'If I had known the temper of the English some years past as well as I do now', she sighed, 'I had never been obliged to quit this house.' When she stepped into her once-beautiful chapel, she found that a plain wooden pulpit and pews had been installed by the congregation of French Protestants who had been using it as their church. She gave orders at once for it to be restored to its former glory.

Less easy to remedy was the problem of James. The fact that Sir Edward Hyde was equally distressed was no consolation. She refused to receive his daughter and when Charles urged her to recognise the marriage, she declared that she would rather go back to France and began to pack up for her departure. Before she and Minette could leave, fresh disaster struck. Princess Mary fell ill and smallpox was diagnosed. Her condition did not seem serious, and indeed she may only have been suffering from measles, but her doctors were determined to bleed her because everyone thought their failure to bleed Henry had led to his death. She was far too weak to withstand the treatment, and she died on Christmas Eve.

Shaken by her loss, Henrietta finally agreed to see James and his wife. On 1 January 1661, dozens of ladies and gentlemen pushed their way into her bedchamber to witness the reconciliation. Anne knelt before her, she bent to kiss her daughter-in-law, then Minette followed suit. The following day she sat next to Anne at dinner and agreed to be the baby's godmother. After the meal, she and Minette left for Portsmouth. The visit had, after all, been only a temporary one and Philip was sending impatient messages from France. They dared not stay away any longer.

As usual, Henrietta's voyage had its dramas. It was a bad time of year for travelling and violent storms blew up. Minette was dreadfully seasick and they had to put back into port. They set off again when it was calmer, only to discover that the Princess had a rash. Could it be smallpox? Henrietta was thrown into a panic. Back they went to land again. Mercifully, the doctors assured them that it was only measles but they had to endure a boring stay in the town before they could leave once more.

Finally, they made the crossing, to find Philip and Louis XIV waiting on the other side. He embraced his bride tenderly, listened with rapt attention to her animated description of all her tribulations and then carried her off to Paris. They were married eight weeks later in Henrietta's chapel in the Palais Royal. So loath was Minette to part from her mother that she stayed on for another few days, before they finally said farewell amid floods of tears and promises of frequent visits.

While Henrietta lived quietly at Colombe, Minette revelled in all the excitement of the French court. Until now, she had led a sheltered life. As Duchess d'Orleans, Philip's wife, she became rather too popular, for she attracted the attention of the King himself. To the fury of Philip, the young Queen Marie Thérèse and the old Queen, Louis XIV began to flirt with her and it seemed to his irate relatives that the flirtation was in danger of turning into a passionate love affair. They remonstrated with Minette to no avail, so they summoned Henrietta to hear their complaints and it took all her famous tact to placate them. They finally accepted that Minette was innocent of any desire to lure Louis away, she and Philip were reconciled, and that winter she announced that she was pregnant.

Henrietta looked forward to the baby's birth with pride and anxiety. Minette had always been delicate. She was dreadfully thin even now, she had a cough and she would obviously need great care. Henrietta was therefore considerably disturbed when Charles II sent messages insisting that his mother come and live permanently in England. She could not possibly leave Paris until her grandchild was born, she said, and then of course when the baby girl was safely delivered she wanted to stay and admire her. She might have lingered longer, but suddenly there was a new incentive to go back to London. Charles had decided to take a wife at last, and Henrietta was determined to see the new Queen of England for herself.

She set out for London once more, this time with the expectation of staying there permanently, and she was gratified to discover that her new daughter-in-law was delightful: she could not have chosen a more suitable girl herself. The Portuguese Catherine of Braganza was gentle, dark-eyed and devout. She had also fallen deeply in love with her husband and when she found out that she would always have to take second place to his mistresses she was wretchedly upset. Henrietta, with her knowledge of the world and her understanding of human nature, helped to reconcile her to her situation, and the two Queens became the best of friends.

Henrietta took up residence at Somerset House. Among her officials were such familiar figures as Lord Jermyn, her Lord Chancellor and Lord Steward; his assistant, Abraham Cowley the poet; Monsieur de Ventelet, with her since her childhood; the erratic Sir Kenelm Digby; Sir John Wintour, her chief secretary from before the Civil War, and the Duchess of Richmond and Lady Denbigh. There were gentlemen ushers and pages, grooms and cupbearers, musicians, footmen, bargemen and chamberwomen. In short, she was surrounded by a complete court of her own and soon people were saying that it was merrier and more welcoming than the King's.

As energetic as ever, she got out old plans Inigo Jones had drawn in 1638 for improvements to the palace, gave orders for the splendid new gallery to be built and laid out an Italian garden. Inigo himself was dead now, but she loved to entertain other old friends. Perhaps Sir Jeffrey Hudson the dwarf visited her. He was back in England, living quietly in the country on a pension from Charles II. Sometimes she went to see round fine houses near the city, spending one afternoon with John Evelyn at Sayes Court. He noted in his journal that she kept the entire company entertained with stories of all the clever things her dogs had done.

Her kindness and her charitable activities were well known, so when a young Chinese stowaway was found on a ship in London, the authorities

143. *Louis XIV and his Family*,
by Jean Nocret. Henrietta is on
the extreme left, as Queen of
the Sea. Philip (Pluto) is next
to her, with Minette (Flora)
beside him. The stout lady in
the centre is Anne of Austria,
Louis XIV (Apollo) is to her
right and his wife Marie
Thérèse is on the right, in
front, as Juno. The lady
standing on the extreme right
is Gaston's daughter.
(Versailles: photograph,
Lauros-Giraudon)

144. *Catherine of Braganza*,
Charles II's Queen, painted by
or after Dirk Stoop, about the
time of her wedding.
(National Portrait Gallery, London)

145. One of a pair of oak cabinets veneered in *lignum vitae*, each decorated with ninety-eight silver plaques, two of which have Henrietta's monogram. They are believed to have been given by her to Henry Jermyn. (Reproduced by gracious permission of Her Majesty The Queen)

knew where to take him. He was brought to Henrietta, who immediately employed him in her household. When she discovered that he could speak English, she told Father de Gamache to give him religious instruction, and she acted as his godmother when he was baptised in her chapel.

Full though her life was, she still missed Minette badly and she was increasingly troubled with bronchitis. She began to long for France and in the spring of 1665 she decided to visit her homeland, ostensibly to take the waters at Bourbon. Her real purpose was to see how Minette was faring. In the past three years she had suffered a serious miscarriage and given birth to a shortlived son and a stillborn daughter. Moreover, there were alarming rumours that Philip was pathologically jealous, declaring to everyone that he hated his wife but causing dreadful scenes whenever any other man spoke to her. When Henrietta arrived back in Paris, she did what she could to smooth over their problems, but it was very difficult.

Louis XIV presented her with a sumptuous town residence, the Hôtel de Bazinièrc, but she spent most of her time quietly at Colombe. She had brought furnishings over from Somerset House and her mansion was famous for its elegance. Her bedchamber was hung with grey damask fringed with gold and silver, with a matching bed. She kept her valuables in beautiful tortoiseshell and *lignum vitae* cabinets and on a table stood her silver-gilt dressing set.

In the little room next door she kept her three china teapots inlaid with silver and two earthenware ones decorated with gold. Tea was an excellent cure for the cold, she had once told Christine. Throughout the house were fine statues, valuable cups, carved agates and ornate boxes. Religious paintings and portraits hung on her walls: pictures of her own parents, her brother Gaston, Anne of Austria, her children, of course, and even a portrait of her favourite dog.

She began each day with a reading from *The Imitation of Christ* and then her time was carefully divided between religious devotions, meals, business and entertainment. She was in bed each night by ten. She did not go much to court, for many of those she had known were gone. Her brother Gaston and Anne of Austria died during these years as did her faithful correspondent Christine, and in any event her own health would not permit strenuous activity. When Charles decided to make war on France, he urged her to come back to London but she refused. She wanted to end her days in Colombe.

He was displeased, and in the winter of 1668, when he was having to economise, he decided to reduce her revenues from her English lands by one quarter. She was deeply hurt. She had already retrenched as much as possible, she protested. Surely he would not 'wish to render the rest of my days, which will be short, unfortunate, by the debts for which I stand engaged'. 'What touches my heart most', she said,' is that people see that your saving extends to your mother'.

That spring she was often ill, troubled with bronchitis, fever, insomnia and fainting fits, but she never spoke of her troubles and Father de Gamache often heard her say that 'complaints in illness were useless, or if they served for anything, it was to show the great weakness and irresolution of the persons who made them'.

She felt a little better when the good weather came, and she was diverted by the arrival of one of her grandchildren, James's daughter, Anne. The four-year-old was very shortsighted, and Henrietta wanted her to be seen by a Parisian eye-specialist. In August Minette gave birth to another daughter, also called Anne, and Henrietta was able to go and visit her at St Cloud. Philip was there too, and as usual he was at his most charming with his mother-in-law. He expressed concern about her health, and he and Minette urged her to see a group of royal doctors. She had no desire to do so, but to please them she agreed.

Monsieur Vallot, the King's principal physician, Monsieur Esprit, Philip's doctor, and Monsieur Ivelin, Minette's medical adviser, arrived at Colombe on Saturday, 8 September. Father de Gamache was present during their consultation and so too was Henrietta's own physician, Monsieur Duquesne. His presence was hardly necessary, for as soon as the visitors began their questions Henrietta launched into a graphic description of all her symptoms and he had no chance to say anything. When she had finished, he did manage to outline the treatment he had been giving, and they nodded their approval. Only Monsieur Vallot had any contribution to make: he suggested that when Henrietta could not sleep, she should take three grains of an opiate.

At that, Henrietta gave a cry of dismay. Dr Mayerne had always advised her against opiates, she said. He had warned her that they were dangerous for her. Monsieur Vallot replied stiffly that he would not have suggested them had he not thought they would help. The others hastily agreed, Monsieur Ivelin adding that although he did not know their ingredients, anything suggested by Monsieur Vallot was bound to be efficacious.

The doctors went back to Paris and Henrietta spent the following day in religious devotions, for she intended to take communion on Monday. On

146. *Queen Anne*, Henrietta's granddaughter, as a child. This picture was painted by Lely about 1667.
(Reproduced by gracious permission of Her Majesty The Queen)

Sunday evening she was as lively as ever, regaling her companions over supper with amusing anecdotes and laughing and joking as though nothing ailed her. She retired to bed, as she always did, at about ten o'clock.

Her doctor asked her if she would have the laudanum, but she was reluctant and he decided that she was too warm to take it. Ordering her attendants to close her bedcurtains, she sent them all away, except for the lady who slept in her chamber. After she had lain awake for an hour or so, she told her lady to summon Dr Duquesne. She would take the grains after all, she said. He was doubtful, but she insisted, so he mixed them up in the yolk of an egg and gave it to her. She drank it, lay back against her pillows and soon she was asleep.

Dr Duquesne sat by her bed. A little later her breathing altered and he saw that she had fallen into a very deep sleep. When he felt her pulse, he found to his dismay that it was alarmingly irregular. Her lady came to bend anxiously over the bed and they both tried to rouse her, but she slept on. The lady ran away to summon help and almost at once her priests and her other doctors were crowding into the room. They all spoke to her, the physicians taking her pulse and trying to question her, the priests exhorting her to confess her sins or at least give some sign that she understood. Some of the doctors believed it was merely a temporary loss of consciousness, but Father de Gamache realised that it was much more serious and he sent for the curé to administer the last rites. Between three and four in the morning, Henrietta died, 'with great serenity and a sweet expression of countenance'.

The following morning, Henry Jermyn wrote to announce the news to Charles II. The members of the little household were all in great distress, he said. Their Queen had been ill for a long time, it was true, but no one had expected her sudden death. If only the wretched doctor had not advised laudanum, she would not have died, they told each other, and they shouted and shook their fists at Monsieur Vallot when he came to call.

To add to their grief they were worried about the practical arrangements. Although Henrietta had left no will in the castle, they knew that she wanted all her property to go to Charles II. Unfortunately, Minette's husband had other ideas. Declaring that his wife was the sole heir, Philip ordered Henrietta's belongings to be sealed up so that no one could take anything away. There was also the problem of the funeral. No one knew who would pay for it, and it would be very expensive, for they had heard that it would be a state occasion. They were much relieved when Louis XIV finally announced that he would take care of everything.

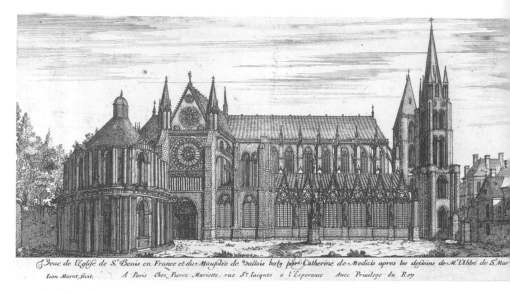

147. *The Abbey of St Denis*, where Henrietta and Minette are buried, engraved by Jean Marot. (Bibliothèque Nationale, Paris)

On the day after her death, Henrietta's body lay on her bed and her attendants were allowed in to make their farewells. The next day, she was embalmed, and then taken to lie in state at Chaillot. Her funeral took place on 12 September at St Denis. An imposing temporary mausoleum had been erected in the choir. In the shape of an octagon, it had eight magnificent marble pillars bearing her arms. Between the columns were draperies of cloth of silver and black, above was a dome of gilded copper with statues, urns and torches and the whole structure was surmounted by a globe supporting a replica of the crown of England. Outside the main edifice four tall pyramids bearing fleurs-de-lys were guarded by life-size white marble figures of the four virtues. Henrietta's body, covered by a brocade cloth, lay beneath the dome.

The congregation began to take their places at ten o'clock in the morning, led by the members of the Paris *parlement* and other government officials. The ambassadors of Venice and Savoy followed, then the members of the Queen's own household, led by the Duchess of Richmond. A hundred poor men clad in grey cloth for the occasion were followed by twenty-four criers, ringing bells. The heralds came next, then Henry Jermyn, dressed like a Capuchin for all he was a Protestant. Immediately behind him were the principal mourners, Minette and her husband. She wore a mantle with a train seven ells long. Philip conducted her to her seat, bowed to the altar and to the dead Queen, then he too took his place.

The Archbishop of Rheims, clad in pontifical vestments, celebrated the Mass, assisted by four bishops, with the royal choristers providing the beautiful music. Minette knelt to kiss her mother's ring, which was held in front of her on a cushion, and Henrietta's coffin was lowered into a vault beside her father by four gentlemen of her chamber. The Archbishop prayed, the captain of her guard threw down his flag into the vault and ceremonially broke his baton of office. His lieutenant and Henrietta's first master of household did likewise. Henry Jermyn handed her crown to one of the heralds, who went down into the vault and laid it on her coffin.

*Mausolée qui a esté faict par ordre du Roy   aux obseques et pompes funebres de la Reyne de
la Grande Bretaigne, en l'Eglise de l'ab-   baye de S.<sup>t</sup> Denis en France le 20. Nouembre 1669.*

I. Marot inv. et fecit

148. *Henrietta's Mausoleum*, a temporary structure erected in St Denis for her funeral;
engraved by Jean Marot.
(Bibliothèque Nationale, Paris)

145

When it was all over, Henrietta's household returned sadly to Colombe. At the end of the month, Charles II's representative arrived to list everything: the fine furniture, the costly ornaments, Henrietta's day clothes and her night-clothes, her few remaining pearls and amethysts, her great diamond cross and the precious little box in her cabinet containing the miniature of Charles I. It was the only picture of him in the house, and it was kept beside 'two rings which are believed to be the Queen's wedding rings'. All the paintings which were not fixed to the walls were to be sent to Charles. The members of the household were allowed to take small keepsakes: the Duchess of Richmond chose a teapot and a little gold cup. Everything else was to be left where it was, for Minette.

Henry Jermyn returned to London to spend his last years in enjoyable card-playing and profitable dealings in the property market. The Duchess of Richmond became one of Catherine of Braganza's ladies-in-waiting. Some of the household remained in France, while others went back to their families. Minette was to die of peritonitis the following year, but in the nine remaining months of her life she mourned her mother deeply. She arranged a special memorial service at Chaillot. The famous preacher Bishop Bossuet gave a stirring oration and Henrietta's heart was buried in the convent chapel. Engraved upon its silver casket was a proud and fitting epitaph: 'Henrietta Maria, Queen of England, France, Scotland and Ireland, daughter of the King of France Henry IV the Victorious, wife of Charles I the Martyr and mother of the restored King Charles II'.

# FURTHER READING

*T*HE MOST direct source for Henrietta's life is her voluminous correspondence. Selections have been printed in English in Mary Anne Green, *Letters of Queen Henrietta Maria* (1857) and in French in Charles, Comte de Baillon, *Lettres de Henriette-Marie, Reine d'Angleterre* (Paris 1877). Hermann Ferrero, *Lettres de Henriette-Marie à sa soeur Christine* (Rome 1881) records the affectionate relationship between the two sisters but adds little of substance.

Two lively works by Louis Batiffol provide valuable background information about Henrietta's childhood in France: *La Vie Intime d'une Reine de France* (Paris 1911) is a biography of her mother, and *Le Louvre sous Henri IV et Louis XIII* (1930) analyses the organisation of Marie de Medici's principal palace. The royal children's home at St Germain, mainly before Henrietta's birth, is described in Lucy Crump, *Nursery Life 300 Years Ago* (1929), based on the diary of Louis XIII's doctor, Jean Héroard, *Journal sur l'Enfance et la Jeunesse de Louis XIII* ed. E Soulie and E de Barthélemy (Paris 1868).

The manuscript listing Henrietta's trousseau is preserved in the Bibliothèque Nationale, Paris, f2, 23600, and a printed pamphlet describes her wedding: *L'Ordre des cérémonies observés au mariage du roy de la Grande Bretagne* (Paris 1625). Her initial difficulties with Charles and Buckingham are recounted by her Lord Chamberlain, Leveneur de Tillières, in his *Mémoires*, edited by M C Hippeau (Paris 1862) and by the Marshal de Bassompierre in his *Journal de Ma Vie: Mémoires*, edited by M J A La Cropte (Paris 1870–77). Father de Gamache was with the Queen for most of her adult life, and he noted her reactions to her dramatic adventures in *Memoirs of the Mission in England of the Capuchin Friars of the Province of Paris from the years 1630–69*, published as volume ii of Thomas Birch, *The Court and Times of Charles I* (1848). Further eyewitness accounts of her doings are to be found in the *Calendar of State Papers Domestic* and the *Calendar of State Papers Venetian*.

Henrietta's relationship with her husband is vividly demonstrated in *Charles I in 1646: Letters of Charles I to Queen Henrietta* edited by John Bruce (The Camden Society 1856), and his theories of kingship are analysed in Stephen Orgel and Roy Strong, *Inigo Jones. The Theatre of the Stuart Court* (University of California). Among recent biographies of Charles, Pauline Gregg, *King Charles I* (1981) and Charles Carlton, *Charles I, the Personal Monarch* (1983) are perceptive and entertaining, the former providing an excellent bibliography for those who wish to study further the Civil War and the political events of the period.

Henrietta's tribulations in Holland can be followed in the Baron Van Heenvliedt's dispatches in *Archives ou Correspondence Inédit de la Maison d'Orange Nassau*, volume ii (Utrecht 1859), while Bernard Morel *The French Crown Jewels* (Antwerp 1988) traces the fate of some of the gems she pawned there. Her own description of, for example, her dreadful voyage back to England, was noted down by Françoise Bertaut, Madame de Motteville, and incorporated in her *Mémoires sur Anne d'Autriche et Sa Cour* (Paris, n.d.).

*Rélation de la pompe funèbre, faite en l'Eglise de S. Denys en France, pour la Reyne Mère d'Angleterre* (Brussels, n.d.) describes Henrietta's funeral; the inventory of her belongings at Colombe is in the Public Record Office, London, SP78/128, and the sermon preached at her memorial service at Chaillot is in Jacques Bossuet, *Oraisons Funèbres* (Paris n.d.).